POSTERS OF THE BELLE EPOQUE

The Wine Spectator Collection

POSTERS
OF
THE BELLE EPOQUE

The Wine Spectator Collection

Jack Rennert

PUBLISHED BY
WINE SPECTATOR PRESS
NEW YORK

DISTRIBUTED BY
THE POSTER ART LIBRARY
A DIVISION OF
POSTERS PLEASE, INC.
NEW YORK

ACKNOWLEDGMENTS

The assistance and generosity of many individuals proved invaluable in producing this volume. In listing some, I run the risk of omitting others, but it's a chance I'll have to take.

First and foremost, I am immensely grateful and honored for the confidence and the friendship of Mr. Marvin R. Shanken. He has given me full rein in the selection of posters as well as the editorial and production aspects of the book. I can only hope that the finished product merits that confidence. His assistant, Ms. Mel Mannion, was helpful in countless ways in the logistics and administration of this book as well.

At the offices of Posters Please, Inc., I had the able assistance of my editor, Mr. Chester Collins, as well as our administrator, Ms. Terry Shargel.

Research assistance and information came from sources too numerous to acknowledge here, but I do want to single out the helpfulness of Mr. Mathias Papon and Ms. Sophie Guinot in Paris as well as Mr. F. Ghozland in Toulouse.

The design and production of the book was handled in a most capable and timely fashion by the firm of Harry Chester, Inc., and I am most grateful to Mr. Michael Mendelsohn, its director, as well as Mr. Alexander Soma, Mr. Crawford Hart, Ms. Susannah Ing and Mr. Tony Hom. Mr. Robert Mauriello also looked over my shoulder and his suggestions have made this a better book.

The book's appearance owes much not only to the artists represented in it but also to the printer I was fortunate to have: Dai Nippon Printing Co. I thank especially Mr. Mutoshi Sakuta and his staff in Tokyo with whom I had the pleasure of working, as well as Mr. Kimio Honda of their New York office. Their careful attention to my many demands showed a caring and a professionalism that sets a standard to be emulated in this field.

All color plates in this book are from the Wine Spectator Collection and all were photographed by Mr. Kent Hanson. Poster insets in black and white are from the Poster Photo Archives division of Posters Please, Inc. All others are credited as shown.

J.R.

Published by
WINE SPECTATOR PRESS
a division of
M. SHANKEN COMMUNICATIONS, INC.
387 Park Avenue South
New York, New York 10016

Distributed by:
THE POSTER ART LIBRARY
a division of
POSTERS PLEASE, INC.
601 West 26 Street, New York, N.Y. 10001
Tel: (212) 787-4000   Fax: (212) 604-9175   email: jrennert@angel.net

Library of Congress Catalogue Card No: 90-060771
ISBN   0-9664202-1-7

Second Printing, May 1999
Printed and bound in Japan by Dai Nippon Printing Co.

TABLE OF CONTENTS

PREFACE

Art critics beware, this book was not created for you. It was created for people like me. People who lack the training in art, but possess the curiosity, and yes, fascination that belle epoque posters evoke.

My affair with posters came about by accident. Twenty years ago, I began collecting turn-of-the-century magazine ads for wine and spirits products, a logical extension of my publishing business. It was an experience that helped teach me about the history of advertising, marketing and brand name building at its earliest stage.

Ten years later, I came across some interesting posters, and immediately felt an excitement that made my heart pound. Posters from the same period as the magazine ads represented an advertising medium a thousand times more powerful. I was hooked, without knowing quite what hit me.

I was swept away by the magnetic force of posters—travel, bicycles, cars, cabaret actors, books, festivals, you name it.

In the beginning my efforts were small and safe. In talking with dealers, the only readily available source for information at the time, I learned that Jules Chéret was "the father of the poster." So that's where I began. My initial purchases were $50, $75, $100 posters, an astronomical amount when compared to my earlier 50-cent up to two-dollar magazine acquisitions. As the bug got more deeply embedded in my psyche, my forays into the unknown world of dealers, galleries, and poster auctions became more frequent and more venturesome.

Early on, I learned that the source for many classic posters sold by American dealers were the flea markets of Paris. Off I went. My wife Hazel by this time realized that I was out of control, but rather than discourage me, she often accompanied me on my buying trips. We had fun together.

Over the years, I began to read everything I could get my hands on—which wasn't much. I talked with everyone and anyone in the poster business who would speak to me, visited museums worldwide, galleries, the homes of private collectors—anywhere, everywhere.

Over time, my taste in posters became more defined.

As I look back now at the collection, of which the best examples are illustrated in this book, I find it hard to believe that anyone (let alone me!), was able to assemble such an array of beautiful works. I wonder whether today, even with a considerable budget, someone could duplicate it. Some of the more important pieces, because of scarcity, took years of searching before they could be acquired.

The hallmark of this poster collection is that the condition of most of the works is far better than you'll find in museums. Early on, I realized that condition, as with wine, coins and other collectibles, was a crucial factor. I let all the dealers know I would pay a premium for mint-condition posters.

One of my dreams is some day to arrange a series of public exhibitions so that this beauty and fun can be shared with others. Already, many of these posters are on display in my New York office and home. Every day they bring me immense visual pleasure and thrill, and I am proud to know my staff works in an esthetically charged ambiance.

Let me here thank my associate, Mel Mannion, for her active involvement, administration and sincere efforts to keep me under control.

If you enjoy the beauty, color and uncompromising style that these poster artists created, you will, I hope, share with me the joy of this book.

Marvin R. Shanken
Editor and Publisher
The Wine Spectator

ABOUT THIS COLLECTION

At first glance, it is hard to find the proper focus on the Wine Spectator collection of posters. If we view it as a wine connoisseur's collection, it doesn't deal with its subject thoroughly enough; if we see it as a general collection, it has too much emphasis on wines and liquors. For a *belle epoque* collection, it has too many posters from other periods; and from any viewpoint, it has altogether too many Cappiellos.

Over a quarter-century of laboring, with love, in the world of posters, it has been one of my pleasures to build spectacular collections for clients from all walks of life, including celebrities, art lovers, people who invest in art, and assorted other poster fans; even some museums, institutions and business corporations. In each case, we start by discussing in depth the ultimate goal of our effort, the exact scope and focus of the intended final result. After that, the happy hunt is on, limited only by time, budget and availability of the posters we want.

In this case, honesty compels me to admit that my input has been somewhere between modest and minimal, and yet somehow despite that, and despite all the demerits I've pointed out, this is an impressive and powerful collection. Marvin Shanken achieved, almost entirely on his own, what often takes me years and a diligent application of all my expertise to produce—namely, a collection that accurately and beautifully reflects, and is an extension of, the personality of its owner.

Yes, he has done exactly that. As a wine expert and publisher he devotes a good amount of attention to posters for spirits and wines. But he is a man of many interests, and all of them are expressed through his acquisitions: he obviously likes the *belle epoque*, but not exclusively so, and he is a great fan of Cappiello; there's nothing wrong with having a personal favorite. But above all, he appreciates beauty, of whatever vintage and style: this collection has the cream of the crop, and that is its strength and its real focus. The real afficionado unhesitatingly takes whatever gives him esthetic pleasure, regardless whether it fits a preconceived pigeonhole of style or subject; and if he's completely honest and follows his impulses, eventually what he amasses establishes its own standards and values. Best of all, it will not owe anything to anybody: it will stand on its own and give testimony about its creator's character.

As Marvin Shanken convincingly demonstrates, the outcome can be breathtakingly powerful, even hauntingly fascinating.

This book does not contain the entire collection, which would have been simply too bulky; besides, it is being constantly added to and changed. However—and here, at last, I can claim to have had something to contribute—we have made a sincere effort to spotlight every facet of it, in approximately the same proportion of artists, subjects and styles as can be found in its totality. As *la belle epoque* is clearly a major area of interest, we have turned our attention to it in the essay which follows, especially since an awareness of the historic background does enhance our pleasure in looking at these century-old posters.

But the collection is neither limited to the *belle epoque* nor does it pretend to be the last word on it. Don't look for any absolutes here: do, however, look for the pure pleasure of enjoying lovely posters. If the collection is the last word on anything, it is on Marvin Shanken—and that's as it ought to be.

Jack Rennert

THE BELLE EPOQUE

Any collection of posters that purports to show the best flowering of pictorial advertising art must necessarily be firmly anchored in the 1890s, and most of its prize items will be French. This is not to imply that poster art was born, full-blown, in Paris at that time; posters existed long before that, in virtually all of the civilized world. Some of them, in fact, especially the early British and American ones, were technically superior to anything being done in France. But they were so relentlessly functional, with heavy emphasis on letterpress text, and so hopelessly bogged in the naive realism of the illustrative style, that to call them art would be stretching a point.

Advertising by means of posters was actually developed elsewhere. In the United States, already in the 18th century there were political placards, posters advertising slave auctions, and traveling circuses and minstrel shows using printed material affixed to walls; for the most part, they were little more than letterpress or wood block announcements with fancy borders. In England, railroad stations were full of posters by the middle of the 19th century: again, they were heavy on fare and schedule information, with artwork only incidental. The same was true everywhere; in his 1896 work on the subject, Ernest Maindron remarks that he found the early German posters, for example, "too cold and heavy-handed."

In France, however, for a variety of reasons, the situation was different. Inspired perhaps by the ostentation and opulence of their monarchs, the French developed a keener sense of art and style than any of their neighbors; Paris became a center of culture and artistic excellence, earning the nickname of "the capital of the 19th century."

As can be expected, the intellectual atmosphere of the city spilled over among the general population. Commerce and industry produced new wealth which created a solid middle class: for the first time in history, the average citizen had discretionary income, leisure, mobility, and access to consumer goods and services never before available. People could afford to develop tastes and to indulge them.

In order to take advantage of the opportunities offered by the new industrial age, people had to acquire skills and upgrade their educational standards. As a byproduct, they developed intellectual curiosity and an appetite to enjoy pastimes. They became avid readers, theatergoers, music and art lovers; such pleasures, previously enjoyed only by a few aristocrats, were rapidly becoming available to anyone.

It was literature, which flourished during these times, that was indirectly responsible for the infusion of art into posters. In the 18th century, French publishers started the trend to have their books lavishly illustrated, and their covers were often fine examples of decorative art. From there, it was but a short step to announce the forthcoming publication of a book by reproducing one of the illustrations—or having one drawn specially for the purpose—and putting it on a placard so that booksellers could display it in their store windows. Small as they were, these cardboards were posters.

This was a radical departure from the prevalent practice of other advertisers who essentially ordered their posters from printers; from them, they could expect little more than the required text in large letters and a few ornamental curlicues. The book illustrators, on the other hand, were usually well established artists; thus, the first posters with any real art in them were essentially book posters.

The critic J.K. Huysmans called posters "the journalism of painting," an often uneasy marriage between the needs of esthetic expression and the needs of everyday communication. Both needs grew in direct relation to the progress of industrialization, which on the one hand created much depressing drabness, which tended to make the gap between life and art so palpable it badly needed some relief, and on the other it created prosperity, which led to a consumer-oriented economy that needed a medium to reach masses of people with product information. The poster filled the bill admirably.

THE PERVASIVENESS OF THE POSTER

As already noted, in the age before mass media like radio, film and TV, the best way to find out what was going on was to be out there where it was happening. People spent much more of their life in the streets; hence, to reach them, advertisers covered every space they could with their messages, as these pictures clearly show.

Kiosks served many purposes, besides the sale of newspapers and magazines. They also afforded the opportunity for billposters to paste their wares—not to mention the fact that they provided a source of revenue to the city. Seen here is a Cote d'Azur poster by Hugo d'Alesi ca.1898. (Photo: Roger Viollet, Paris).

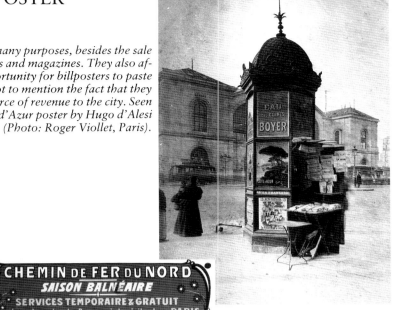

Of several recognizable posters on this 1898 Paris wall, the most important is Mucha's Waverley Cycles, as well as four copies of the large Columbia Chainless poster by Romes. (Photo: Roger Viollet, Paris).

The French railways provided free pick-up and delivery services of trunks of vacationing Parisians using their services. Of course, they did not fail to put their own railway posters on the sides of their carriages. (Photo: Mme Florence Camard, Paris).

And if the outdoors did not provide enough opportunity, the message could move indoors as well: here we see a screen in a French apartment in 1899 which used four of Mucha's posters for Sarah Bernhardt for decor. (Photo: Etude Daussy-Ricqlès, Paris).

In this 1903 Paris photo, we can identify Privat Livemont's Automobile Club de France poster, as well as that for Bon Marché by J. Wagner, on the walls of the Cremerie. (Photo: Library of the City of Paris).

On the front of the building of the Manufactures des Tabacs on rue de l'Université, we spot some automobile posters, including L'Auto-Palace (by Grün?). (Photo: Library of the City of Paris).

For mass communication to be feasible, it has to be loud, colorful, and easy to disseminate. In a poster, loudness means making it big enough to notice and easy to read; colorfulness is self-explanatory; and for "easy to disseminate," read "cheap." Fortunately for posters, the printer's craft came up, at the end of the 18th century, with the answer: lithography.

Until then, the standard techniques to reproduce line drawings in a size larger than a book page involved the use of woodcuts or copper engravings; both were rather expensive and limited as to size. Few advertisers wanted to spend that kind of money: those who did amortized their investment over a period of time; for example, a theater would print a large amount of stock posters with only its name on it and some artwork to serve as a marquee, then imprint a few at a time with the name of the current show, which could be done anywhere on a letterpress.

It was, in fact, an impoverished actor who gave advertising by posters a decisive boost. Aloys Senefelder (1771–1834), born in Prague, tried his hand at the theatrical craft, both as actor and unsuccessful playwright, but didn't make much headway. Deciding that the only way to get his work before the public was to print it himself, he tried to obtain the necessary plates, but found that they were too expensive. It occurred to him the if he used cheap limestone instead of metal, he might be able to scrape the money together; apparently, he was aware of the principle on which his innovation was based, namely the simple fact that a layer of grease on a stone will protect it from corrosion.

After some experimenting, he first demonstrated his invention in 1798 by printing the musical score of some works by a man who helped him financially in his struggle. Called lithography, the new printing method used, in place of metal or wood plates, flat slabs of limestone ground to a perfectly even surface. The desired image is drawn on the stone with a grease pencil, and then the plate is subjected to an acid bath; this will eat away a thin layer of the stone everywhere except where the pencil marks protect it. All that is needed after that is to affix the slab to a printing press, apply some ink and bring it in contact with a sheet of paper: the greased portions of the stone will leave their imprint. After printing, the stone can be scrubbed clean and made even again, so that the same plate can be used many times until it wears too thin or uneven. For printing in color, a separate stone is used for each inking.

By the 1830s, lithography was well established as a technique for printing large notices and posters. The best craftsmen and largest presses were found in England and in the United States; circuses, in particular, became early customers for billboard-size publicity, favoring huge letters and loud colors. It didn't matter if the drawing was crude; certainly no one would have dreamt of claiming that a notice which would be destroyed by the elements in a few days or weeks had any pretensions of art.

And yet it was a few samples of these primitive American show posters that inspired a young French printer's apprentice to add the one element that was still missing—artistic imagination. Jules Chéret was still in his teens in the 1850s when he saw the large showbills at one of the world fairs which were held every few years during this time. This being the age of technology in which every new development was hailed by a progress-minded population, fairs at which advances in science and industry were proudly shown off became regular events. It occurred to Chéret, as he looked at posters bigger and better than anything the printer for whom he was working could produce, that if he learned this new craft in England, he could come back to Paris and improve his prospects immeasurably. The rest is history: through Chéret, the initiative in poster progress passed into French hands.

It should be noted that Chéret, at that time, had never heard of William Morris's arts-and-crafts movement—he couldn't have, as it didn't develop until the 1870s—but the idea of fusing the functional with the esthetic obviously occurred to him just the same.

By the 1870s, Chéret had all the elements of poster art pretty well under control, and was doing more and more posters for show business, which was particularly suited to his bright, airy treatment. He had learned to blend colors and how to achieve every imaginable shade by overprinting and by the spatter technique. He integrated the lettering in the design smoothly—always a tough problem—and harmonized it with the composition.

Around Chéret, the conditions for the flowering of posters kept improving. Paris had begun, in the mid-nineteenth century, an unprecedented rebuilding program which resulted in a carefully laid out network of wide boulevards and spacious vistas. As hundreds of old structures were being demolished to make this possible, Huysmans made the ironic comment that Chéret's posters should be banned as some opponents of outdoor advertising had proposed, because they interfered so much with the monotony of orderly street planning.

LARGE-SCALE POSTER PRINTERS

Looking at pictures of lithographic printing plants from the turn of the century clears up some misconceptions we may have about the way posters were produced.

First of all, we always see tracks, with dollies on it to move the heavy printing stones. They may have been moved by four men up to a certain size, but once they were 120 x 160 cm (47 x 63 in.) or larger, the little conveyance was a must.

Secondly, the posters were obviously not made by hand in some attic: these were large establishments, virtual factories, with assembly line operations.

One thing that may shock us is the tender age of the many apprentices we see in the pictures: child labor laws were still in the future, and we'd hate to know how long these 12- to 14-year-olds had to work.

But through this all, we can't help but admire the delicacy and precision of the finished product: these lumbering machines and unwieldy stones created works of charm and beauty that even the most modern present-day printer need not be ashamed of.

Imprimerie Camis, Paris, ca.1893. On walls can be seen posters by Guillaume and Bouisset, among others.

Imprimerie Camis, Paris, 1894. Again, we see works by Guillaume (Ambassadeurs/Duclerc) and Bouisset (Chocolat Menier), as well as lithographers working on the cumbersome stones.

Imprimerie Paul Dupont, Paris, ca.1893. This is the firm which had Pal under exclusive contract for several years, and so, appropriately, we see several of his posters, including Lucile Wraim on the wall, far right, and his Courses de Spa on the presses.

Imprimerie Karcher, Paris, 1920. Karcher was a job-printer who produced scores of posters for agents and other printers, their name rarely appearing on the printed posters. They printed over 100 posters of Cappiello, both for Vercasson and Devambez, his two agents. (For instance, No. 167, Cognac Pellisson, was in fact printed here.)

Photo Credits: The first top two and the lower left photos are from the book, Les Arts et les Industries du Papier en France 1871–1894, *by Marius Vachon (Librairies-Imprimeries Réunies, Paris, 1894). The photo lower right is from the Karcher printing company's archives in Paris (with special thanks to Mr. Denys Boulenger).*

It became clear that if posters were here to stay, provisions had to be made where to put them. Billboards were one answer; another one, developed originally in England but embraced most enthusiastically in France, were kiosks, which began to make their appearance in the 1840s. Public notice boards had always been a source of revenue to the city; it was therefore decided that posters could be displayed only after they had a tax stamp affixed to them. This, in turn, brought about the standardization of sizes, as the fee was determined by the square footage: new terms, such as "colombier" (61 x 82 cm), "grand aigle" (110 x 70 cm) and "jésus" (70 x 65 cm) came into use. Posters were finding their way into vacant walls, fences, sides of newspaper stands and the ever present pissoirs, and into shop windows.

The true extent of this trend was apparently often underestimated by those living in the midst of it. Two major inventions of the time, the phonograph and the motion picture, were conceived primarily as a means to preserve historic occasions and to facilitate business communications; yet both achieved instant success overwhelmingly as media of popular entertainment. Significantly, in both cases it was also French initiative that put these American inventions on the right track: while Edison was busy recording politician's speeches and arias by opera singers, Charles Pathé made records with popular stars and earned millions; and where cameramen in the rest of the world were busy photographing coronations and processions, Georges Melies made short films using every possible trick the camera was capable of, and popularized the new medium beyond the developer's wildest dreams.

What eventually became known as the *belle epoque*, or the Naughty Nineties, was therefore predominantly a French phenomenon. All the intellectual, social and artistic ferment that characterizes the last few years of the 19th century was present there in a fertile, volatile environment; Paris set the trend in every aspect of popular culture.

In the field of posters, there was already the urgent need of the expanding consumer economy to find a way to communicate; but two more things were needed to elevate posters to a new status and launch the postermania that raged in the brief but crucial period 1895–1900. The first of these was the entry of major artists into the arena; the second was recognition of this fact and its dissemination to the public.

Artists became attracted to posters first in a trickle, then in a flood. The 1880s saw such hesitant newcomers as Grasset and Choubrac; then, in 1891, Bonnard and Toulouse-Lautrec opened the gate wider; when Mucha, Pal and Livemont chimed in with their contributions in 1895, it was evident that no artist need be ashamed to offer his services for commercial use.

A major factor in the popularity of posters in this period is the outdoor-oriented culture. As a generation weaned on television as the most frequent source of entertainment, we cannot truly appreciate how important the outdoor was. As British poster connoisseur James Laver put it: "The 'nineties was a time when, in Paris at any rate, everybody lived in public. Traffic, though brisk, was not yet overwhelming. People had time to stroll, to look about them and, incidentally, to gaze upon that picture-gallery of the boulevard which the poster-hoarding had become. There they saw, fixed for a moment in the eternity of Art, the very life stream which swirled and danced and bubbled around them. Paris lived in public. Many Parisians took all their meals, even the *petit déjeuner*, in one or other of the innumerable cafés which had sprung up everywhere. At the hour of the apéritif half the population was sitting at the little tables on the pavement watching the other half go by." (*XIXth Century French Posters*, London, 1944, p.10).

As to persuading the public to view posters as art, several avenues were used. Yeoman service was performed by the small literary magazines which sprang up like mushrooms after a rain during this turbulent era, and whose editors were keenly alert to everything new. The magazines had, in fact, predisposed the public to accept the artists who would eventually dominate posterism: *Le Chat Noir* was publishing Steinlen and Willette's drawings since 1881; *Le Courrier Français* acquainted its readers with Forain and Metivet from 1884 on; *La Revue Blanche*, *Le Mirliton*, *L'Escarmouche*, and *Le Rire* popularized Toulouse-Lautrec; *Cocorico* and *Quartier Latin* had Mucha. In 1889, *La Plume* opened its Salon des Cent, through which it gave ordinary citizens access to the works of Ensor, Paul, Ibels, and virtually all the posterists active at the time. The *Gil Blas* published more than a thousand Steinlen drawings between 1891 and 1900.

The *belle epoque* fascination with posters was such that a number of magazines sprang up almost simultaneously in different parts of the world in the mid-1890s that were devoted to posters exclusively. There was *L'Estampe et l'Affiche* (1897) in France; two magazines named *The Poster*—one in New York (1896), one in London (1898); *Poster Lore* came into being in

Kansas City (1896); poster fever was at its highest pitch. Significantly, none of these survived more than a year into the new century.

The Salon des Cent epitomizes the second important means of spreading the poster message: making posters available as art for the home. Many major lithography shops started to make it a practice to print a few hundred copies beyond the advertiser's order, and sold them to collectors: among these were Lemercier, Champenois, Vercasson, Ancourt, Chaix and many others in Paris, Cassan Fils in Toulouse, Ricordi in Milan, DeRycker in Brussels.

This brought print dealers into the picture: before long, some of the most prestigious houses were printing catalogues of posters for sale, including Arnould, Pierrefort, Kleinmann, Sagot and others.

Poster exhibitions were, of course, a major step in getting posters recognized. The first traceable one appears to have been staged in Brussels in 1884; in was followed by one in Paris about six weeks later. Chéret was the first, appropriately, to be honored by a one-man exhibition, in 1890 in Paris. The most lavish poster show of the *belle epoque* was the monumental event at Reims in 1896, with well over a thousand items; it is credited with giving poster collecting a decisive push.

Publishers jumped on the bandwagon in the mid-90s. Posters first began to appear as color supplements to periodicals such as *L'Estampe et L'Affiche* or *Le Courrier Français*; the next step was the publication of a monthly portfolio of poster reproductions, such as *Les Maitres de l'Affiche*, selected by one of the early poster chroniclers, Roger Marx, which appeared between 1896 and 1900.

POSTERS AND CENSORSHIP

A

B

C

Although we often see women provocatively posed and scantily dressed in French posters of the Nineties, it must be remembered that artists were toiling under the watchful eyes of censors. How much that affected their designs is difficult for us to say today. We do know that there were instances when they stepped over the boundaries of imposed official taste and incurred the wrath of the censors. One such instance is the censorship we point out in the case of Steinlen's LA TRAITE DES BLANCHES (*See* No. 111).

Another interesting case involved Alfred Choubrac, who in 1891 depicted a girl showing off her charms in a skimpy costume to advertise a new publication titled *Fin de Siècle* (A). A censor objected, whereupon both Choubrac and his publisher refused to redraw the figure or add any more clothing, and instead showed their displeasure by reprinting the poster with the objectionable section duly whited out and overprinted with the explanation that "this portion of the design was censored." (B). Later, Choubrac added his own comment, designing a poster showing a scissor and some leaves and advertising "a fine

selection of fig leaves of all sizes for illustrated posters." (C). To which Maindron concluded, "La vengeance est le plaisir des dieux" (Vengeance is the pleasure of the gods) (p.55).

The censors were apparently not totally autocratic; the light-hearted response of the artists indicates they could be ridiculed with impunity, and so does the fact that print dealers, in these cases, continued to offer both censored and uncensored versions for sale. Victorian prudery may have been the official line, but the public did have choices.

The first spate of books devoted to posters as an art subject appeared in 1895, strangely enough in the United States: "The Modern Poster" by Arsene Alexandre et al., published by Scribner's in New York; "Some Posters," by William T. Higbee, published by the Imperial Press in Cleveland, and "The Reign of the Poster," by Charles K. Bolton, which came out in Boston. The following year saw the publication of Charles Hiatt's "Picture Posters" in London, and of the most serious scholarly work on the subject, by art critic and connoisseur Ernest Maindron, "Les Affiches Illustrées," in Paris—a follow-up to his historic survey of 1886 which bore the same title. In 1897, America was heard from again—"Posters in Miniature," by Percival Pollard, New York—as was Germany—Jean-Louis Sponsel: "Das Moderne Plakat," Dresden—and Belgium—Alexandre D. de Beaumont: "L'Affiche Belge."

As can be seen, the *belle epoque* was virtually saturated with information about posters, and they were easily available in both original size and as reproductions. The wave of enthusiasm for them which swept both Europe and the United States did not last, however, much past the turn of the century; it took several decades and two world wars before posters were again taken up as a legitimate art subject, and began to regain their popularity as art for the home as well as an investment and a collectible item.

That doesn't mean that the poster, per se, withered away in the intervening years. On the contrary, it flourished and went on to become an omnipresent symbol of the 20th century; new artists and new styles came and went, but the basic language of the poster remained unchanging: brisk, direct, functional communication delivered with maximum efficiency to the widest possible audience. It is true that other media, not available to 19th century advertisers, supplemented and, in many cases, supplanted the poster, but they never eliminated the need for it; and quantitatively, at least, there is much more poster activity in the world today than there ever was in the poster heyday of the 1890s.

But never again was there such an era of sheer joyous euphoria in posters, the pleasure of discovering art on street corners and sides of barns, the excitement of reading avidly about the lastest efforts of poster designers…all that has become part of the nostalgic past. It has joined the other things we associate with the *belle epoque*: gaslight and floor-length dresses, Sunday strolls in the park, bicycles built for two, barbershop quartets, handlebar mustaches and bustles. Conditioned largely by period films and romantic literature, we look back at the 1890s as a leisurely, tranquil period in which the Victorian generation moved at a stately pace, doing nothing much and worrying about less. Posters, also, must bear their share of the responsibility for this image we have: they always portray their subjects in perfect comportment and indolent enjoyment.

But then, reflect how little today's advertising image of a sleek car zipping along a gloriously empty mountain road has to do with the reality of day-to-day city traffic, and it is easy to see that the poster world of the 1890s is not the real world of the 1890s, either.

To the person living at the time, the world was, in fact, as complex and confusing as ours is to us today. Technological progress, industrial revolution, social changes, new discoveries were coming up all the time at an accelerated pace. There were conflicts in many parts of the world; there were new political trends, radical factions, women's emancipation, rumblings of the oppressed, monarchies crumbling and republican movements emerging. New modes of transportation, new means of communication were making the world ever smaller, ever more congested, ever faster paced.

Yet what we see, when we look at the way that arts of the era—and posters, of course, are part of it—represent their own time to us, we see the idealized 1890s, the *belle epoque* we are so fond of in our imagination. What they are showing us is, in sober reality, only a small part of the experience of the 1890s, but it is by far the best and most memorable part. The posters show us how the average person spent his leisure—what entertained him, what he wore, how he went about and what he admired. They give us a direct visual link to the past, and often tell us in one glimpse more than a whole text on sociology can convey. To anyone who enjoys a good poster this is the essence of the most democratic of all graphic arts.

THE COST OF A POSTER

When Ernest Maindron wrote his comprehensive treatise on the poster in 1895, he included a charming little chapter on the production and dissemination of posters from the viewpoint of a complete neophyte. It is written in a chatty, unsophisticated style, with imagined conversations and personal comments, but it does convey very effectively the very practical decisions involved in the process of going step by step from the desire

to publicize something to the reality of a poster hanging on a Paris billboard. There is much bewailing of the costs; yet, in the final analysis, that always is a decisive factor, and he makes it painfully clear that it was just as much the crux of the matter when a few centimes were involved as it would be today with hundreds of francs (or dollars) in the balance.

Since Maindron's work was never published in English—and the

French original has long been unavailable—we think it may be worthwhile to present a sampling of his thoughts and ideas exactly as he wrote them a century ago. Through all their quaint naivete we can sense at all times Maindron's genuine liking for the subject and admiration for everyone involved in the detailed mechanics of poster production.

(Les Affiches illustrées 1886–1895, *published in 1896 by G. Boudet, Paris).*

Have you ever thought of following the stages of creating an illustrated poster, from the moment the artist creates the sketch until the day it will be displayed on the walls? You have enjoyed its effect on you; have you asked yourself what has gone into the creation of this effect. Do you know how much it costs?

I shall try to show you.

Let us suppose for a moment that we create together, on the boulevard, in the center of the city, a theater which woud revolutionize the world; if you wish, we shall call it the *Musical and Literary Fantasies*. Our inaugural play requires a sensational poster.

Who will be the lucky artist who will present it to the public?

It is obvious that a poster designed by Mr. A. will be more expensive than one by Mr. B. We know that we could receive better prices from Mr. C. and especially from Mr. D., but I think that it is in our best interest to seek out Mr. A.; his talent is universally appreciated, he is in the public's favor more than any of his competitors.

Our poster, designed by him, will receive everybody's attention; the *Fantasies* will benefit considerably from his personal efforts.

Let us therefore approach Mr. A. [Actually, it becomes clear that, like almost all clients, he is addressing the agent/printer who exclusively represents the artist rather than the artist himself.]

His first question would concern the format of our poster; could it be that this word "format" is not a very precise notion in your mind?

The following table will help us (sizes include margins):

¼ "colombier" is 41 x 30 cm [16⅛ x 11¾ in]
½ "colombier" is 60 x 41 cm [23⅝ x 16⅛ in]
the "jésus" is 70 x 65 cm [27½ x 16⅛ in]
the "colombier" is 61 x 82 cm [24 x 32¼ in]
the "grand-aigle" (big eagle) is 110 x 70 cm [43¼ x 27½ in]
the "double colombier" is 122 x 82 cm [48 x 32¼ in]
the "double grand-aigle" is 140 x 110 cm [55⅛ x 43¼ in]
the "quadruple colombier" is 164 x 122 cm [64½ x 48 in]

the "quadruple grand-aigle" is 220 x 140 cm [86½ x 55⅛ in]

While I am thinking of it, let us determine the value of the tax stamp that would have to be affixed on the poster that we are preparing:

The ¼ "colombier" requires a 6-centimes stamp.
The ½ "colombier" requires a 12-centimes stamp.
The "jésus" and the "colombier" require 18-centimes stamps each.
The other sizes require 24-centimes stamps.

The formats used most frequently are the double and the quadruple colombier. Let me assure you that we should pick the double colombier. On the wall, it is very effective; it has the intimacy of a picture; it is neither too small, nor too big. In a few months, after the *Fantasies* are successfully launched and our profits begin to accrue, we will choose larger formats. For the moment, let us save money; therefore, we will take the double colombier.

Let us be smart. Let us give the artist his creative freedom. We have shown him what we had in mind, and he knows better which nail he should strike; let him use the hammer.

—How much would we have to spend for our poster? We'll start with a modest press run of one thousand copies.

—This would cost one thousand francs, said Mr. A.

—Wow! Each poster would cost one franc? God, this is expensive! We would have saved about one half if we had been dealing with Mr. D.

—You still have time.

—Oh, no, we don't have any time left. Besides, we want a sensational poster, we have decided to revolutionize the world.

—I will help you, Mr. A. said. Why don't you print two thousand copies? Your cost would be thirteen hundred francs, making the price of a single poster just 65 centimes; if you increase your order to three thousand, the unit cost is 52 centimes. Actually, above two thousand, the price is only 250 francs per thousand and this is understandable; the design is finished and the presses are rolling. All we have to do is cover the cost of the paper and of press time. The more you increase the size of your order, the greater the unit price reduction.

—This seems correct. Let us then print three thousand—the deal is made! (However, it still seems expensive!)

After eight days, we can at last take a look at the work.

—It's fine, very good! There is no change to be made. It's perfect. Let me take my original design; we'll place it in full view in our director's office.

—No, said Mr. A.; this maquette is my property. I contracted only to supply you with a printed poster which is similar to this original design that you had approved.

—This maquette is not ours? My God, it is expensive!

—Yes, it is expensive because it is good.

—It certainly is.

—Therefore, it is not expensive.

—Let us leave it like this.

Finally, the printer has finished his work. Our poster is ready. Now we will have to find the poster company which will have it pasted on the walls of the capital.

Choosing such a company is not a casual matter. Let us contact the oldest one in Paris; in addition to being certain that our order will be properly filled, we will have the pleasure of meeting a manager who is very knowledgeable, gracious and polite; no one knows better the difficulties of distributing a poster in a reasonable and useful manner.

If we had to announce the publication of an adventure novel, where the hero kills himself after having taken care of the other characters, we would have our poster distributed in the tenement sections; if we were publicizing a science work, we would place it in the intellectual quarters; if we had to promote an amusement establishment, something like the Moulin Rouge, with its lurid colors and green-tinged lighting, we would turn our backs to the posh Rue Saint-Dominique; if our poster defended the throne and the altar, we would stay away from the socialist-anarchist sector of Belleville.

This is not our case. The shows at the theater which we are going to inaugurate will be attended by those interested in literature or music. The range of our activity is limited.

The greater part of our print run will be displayed on the major thoroughfares or on nearby streets; we will not go beyond the Place de la Madeleine or the Place du Chateau-d'Eau. A certain number of posters will give notice that we are around, and they will be placed just about everywhere. We will hold some in reserve to use later on.

Under these circumstances, since we know that our poster is costing us 52 centimes each, printed, let us see how much this is going to cost us after pasting on the walls.

Here, let us stop for a moment. Let us assume that the *Fantasies* poster, pasted at random at the whim of the billposter, immediately runs the serious risk of being replaced by others pasted over it.

Would we rather have the contracting company guarantee that our poster, which had been conceived with care, carrying our hopes with it, would not succumb to the fate of the streets?

But the unexpected has its charms, and luck could be on our side; let us assume that we are simply putting it up. Since our poster's format is double colombier, a 24-centimes tax stamp would have to be affixed to each poster; to have it pasted on would cost us 15 centimes. Therefore, a poster on the wall would cost us 91 centimes. You can see the difference: if we had printed only 1,000, each piece would have cost 1.39 francs; 2,000 pieces would have cost 1.13 francs each.

Let us take the second case; it merits consideration. Suppose we want to insure that our distribution will be protected from potential obliteration. Therefore, we shall accept the mainte-nance and conservation rates which apply to billboards which are the company's property. This is the operation, separate from the pasting, for which we held a quantity in reserve. It will not be necessary to use up this entire reserve since we will have to replace, at our expense, posters which were spoiled.

Now, the amounts that we will have to spend are substantial.

The cost of the poster is fixed; as we have said, for printing and for the stamp, it comes to 76 centimes.

If we wish to have it preserved and maintained on the company's thousand billboards, we will have to spend the following amounts over the 76 centimes per poster (the 15-centime cost of pasting is included):

for one month, 100 francs.
for three months, 280 francs.
for six months, 550 francs.
for twelve months, 1,000 francs.

Prudently, we shall choose a one-month contract; this will permit us to see how events develop; in any case we will always have the option of extending our contract.

I hope that we will have a hit, so that, emboldened by our success, we will have new and larger posters made after our first favorable experience. The new ones will be quadruple colombiers. It is true that this is going to double the cost of our advertising effort, but what an honor for the *Fantasies!*

. . .

The big billpasting companies are beautifully organized. Until sometime ago they were unknown in their present form; universal suffrage, with its outpouring of political and campaign posters, has brought them prominence, thank God, and since then they have achieved extraordinary progress. They are little known. It's hard to believe how promptly they act, how efficient they are, what a timely service their agents perform. With a single word, they can mobilize an army of workers.

Their intelligent industry does not limit itself to Paris; they spread their brushes to the 78 towns of the Seine district, the 36,000 towns of France and Algeria. They paste as high as a man's height, they paste by ladder, they paste in public conveyances, in buses, in theaters, in municipal buildings, in ferries. Even the smallest unoccupied spot is a part of their domain.

The development of modern advertising has made them real powers. They have superb public relations; they even know politicians!

ARRANGEMENT OF THE BOOK

The reproductions are assorted by artists, who in turn are grouped by stylistic criteria chosen to permit an attempt at classification. The posters were selected from the much larger Wine Spectator Collection with a view toward providing a representative sampling of the art trends from the belle epoque.

Each poster is captioned in the following manner:

Artist
NAME OF POSTER
Year: Printer
Width x height
    (in inches and
    centimeters)
References (list of
    referenced works
    appears at the end
    of the book)

CHERET
AND
HIS COLLEAGUES

From *Le Petit Français illustré*, Easter 1899 issue.

It would be impossible to start a book on turn-of-the-century posters with anyone but the indefatigable pioneer, Jules Chéret, who virtually defined the poster as we know it.

With him, we have grouped a few artists who openly acknowledge their debt to him and could be called his disciples, as well as some others whose relationship to him was less direct but whose designs bear unmistakable signs of his influence. In a larger sense, of course, all posterists owe him a profound debt; this first grouping is simply our arbitrary selection of those who can be termed his colleagues.

JULES CHERET

In 1880, some 10 years before the poster craze got even started, art critic Karl Huysmans made the observation that there was a thousand times more talent in the smallest of Chéret's posters than there was in the majority of the pictures hung at the Paris Salon. He probably meant it mostly to startle some of the "Establishment" painters out of their complacency; it was nevertheless a very perceptive statement about a posterist who was still far from reaching his creative peak. What Huysmans saw is something that breathes from every Chéret poster: a vibrant, dynamic force that virtually compels you to stop, look and be enchanted.

Just how potent that force was can be estimated from Charles Hiatt's assessment, written in 1895: "Many have produced charming wall pictures: nobody, save Chéret, has made an emphatic mark on the aspect of a metropolis. Paris, without its Chérets, would be Paris without one of its most pronounced characteristics; Paris, moreover, with its gaiety of aspect materially diminished. The great masses of variegated colour formed by Chéret's posters greet one joyously as one passes every hoarding, smile at one from the walls of every café, arrest one before the windows of every kiosque. The merits of the Saxoléine lamp, the gaieties of the Moulin Rouge, the charms of Loie Fuller, the value of a particular brand of cough-lozenges are insisted upon with a good-humoured vehemence of which Jules Chéret alone appears to know the secret. Others, in isolated cases, have possibly achieved more compelling decorations, but none can pretend to a success so uniform and so unequivocal."

"Chéret is utterly original," chimes in Charles Matlack Price in 1913, "generally subversive, and sometimes almost exasperating in an audacity which throws all precedent to the winds, and launches lightly clad female figures, floating—ephemeral as so many soap-bubbles, sparkling, iridescent, and explosive. They seem evoked from nothingness, born of daring and fantastic gaiety, and seem joyously to beckon the beholder on with them in a madcap, elusive chase after pleasure."

Jules Chéret (1836–1932), the man who was to exercise such a profound influence on his trade, was born in Paris just about at the time when the first posters produced by the lithographic process were being pasted on the billboards and vacant walls around town. But they were still crude affairs, composed mostly of large type and a few border curlicues; lithography, although available as a technique since 1798, was a slow, clumsy, extremely expensive method of printing, economically impractical for posters. And, in fact, most at this time were printed by metal or wood-block engravings, with some handcoloring added for effect at times.

It was Chéret, the lithographic innovator—he became a printer's apprentice at the age of 13—as well as the artistic and advertising genius, who formulated the technical means to produce posters of every shading of the rainbow with just three or four stones and thus, for the first time, made the color pictorial poster an economically feasible marketing instrument. Moreover, as the little magazine *Poster Lore* stated in 1896, "It was not until Jules Chéret, the magician of the brush, began to design his posters with their startling color effects and odd originality, that poster designing attracted attention as a special branch of art."

He gave posters life and proved they were art; and to top it off, he produced, in a career spanning more than half a century, more of them than anyone else. Lucy Broido, in her definitive 1980 catalogue, lists 1,069 of them; but many of his early ones will probably never be traced. That's a remarkable achievement for any artist, and the fact that in all this prodigious output he managed to maintain a consistent level of inspiration and spontaneity is nothing less than phenomenal. Naturally, in that many designs, he had to hark back to similar themes, yet no Chéret poster is ever dull, stale or lacking in original creative spark.

Chéret's first posters were done for the theater. In 1858 he sold a design for a poster advertising the new light opera, "Orphée aux Enfers," to its composer Jacques Offenbach, allegedly for 100 francs. Encouraged by this, he continued to learn his trade in London, where color lithography was at an advanced stage; he produced some more posters there, and on his return to Paris in 1866 he was ready to open his own printing shop. Almost immediately, he had more commissions from Offenbach, and other theatrical work followed. Magazine and book publishers came next, and by 1881 he was doing so well he merged his operation with a larger printer, Chaix, who thereafter produced all his work.

In the beginning, Chéret based his designs on the illustrative techniques of the day but soon he began to understand that the needs of a poster are different, and evolved his own standards. The mainspring of everything is almost always action—and this he depicted with such irrepressible vitality that it is impossible not to notice it, and once having done so, impossible to ignore it: in most cases, it involved one of his patented soaring beauties. Whatever background and supporting figures are needed are drawn and colored simply to give the design some depth, but never to distract from the central action: the figures are indistinct, the colors have darker tones, perspective is not strictly adhered to, and there are no elaborate details or embellishments.

Chéret was in every way a pioneer, an innovator, a mentor—the prophet of the poster.

1.
Jules Chéret
LE PUNCH GRASSOT
1895: Chaix, Paris
34¼ x 48¼ in./87 x 122.5 cm
Broido, 876
Maitres, 5
DFP-II, 258
PAI-VIII, 150

2. ▶
Jules Chéret
PIPPERMINT
1899: Chaix, Paris
34 x 48¼ in./86.4 x 122.5 cm
Broido, 884
Maitres, 213
PAI-VIII, 146

Two fetching young ladies offer us tempting libations. LE PUNCH GRASSOT is one of the first posters selected for reproduction in the prestigious series *Maitres de l'Affiche,* where it appears as No. 5. In the PIPPERMINT poster, notice how the shadowy blue on the left and the warm orange on the right of the girl's dress subtly evoke the idea that she is sitting by a cozy fireplace, unseen somewhere at right.

In 1796, Jean Get, a young chemist in the town of Revel in the Haute Garonne district near Toulouse, decided to create the ultimate creme de menthe, and gave his product a name which would remind the buyer of the English word "peppermint." It became known later as "Get 27" because it contained 27% alcohol, probably a major reason for its immediate success; only quite recently, in 1976, the company added a second product, popularly known as "Get 31." Meanwhile, the original Pippermint still accounts for some 70% of all creme de menthe sales in France. The headquarters remain in the founder's home town, but since 1969, the company has had a modern corporate structure. The product is also sold, according to their publicity, in 122 countries.

A Chéret classic, glowing with irrepressible zest, is the perfect image for a product which earned much of its renown by clever promotion. This specimen of VIN MARIANI has English text, emphasizing the fact that the company always thought in global terms.

The founder of the enterprise was Angelo Mariani (1838–1914), a native of Corsica who came to Paris at the age of 25 as a humble pharmacist's apprentice. But the young man had ambition, and soon came up with the idea of combining the medicinal properties of coca leaves with his favorite bordeaux, thus coming up with a medicine that didn't taste like one. This was the era when dozens of "tonic wines," "herbal potions" and "stomach bitters" were on the market, all liberally laced with alcohol, so Vin Mariani faced a stiff competition. But it held its own, and in time gained an edge on all of the others—partly because of the intoxicating dash of cocaine in it, but mostly because of Mariani's unexpected talent as a publicist. Long before it became a general practice, he shrewdly recognized the value of celebrity endorsements, and had doctors, musicians, comedians, respected public figures and even some minor royalty praising his tonic in ads and posters.

In 1910, the use of cocaine was discontinued after some customers experienced adverse reactions, but by then the tonic was so well established that it didn't have much effect on sales, and the product remains popular to this day.

3.
Jules Chéret
VIN MARIANI
1894: Chaix, Pairs
34 x 48 ⅜ in./86.3 x 123 cm
Broido, 865
Maitres, 77
Maindron, 731
DFP-II, 148
PAI-VII, 107

4.
Jules Chéret
QUINQUINA
DUBONNET
1895: Chaix, Paris
34½ x 48½ in./87 x 123.2 cm

Broido, 868
Maindron, 733
DFP-II, 252
Maitres, 109
PAI-V, 149

In 1846, Joseph Dubonnet was a wine agent in Paris, representing among others the products of Chartreuse. Medicinal bitters were coming into vogue just then, and he attempted to join the bandwagon with an aperitif based on quinine. After many experiments in his modest quarters near the Opera with the help of his two sons, Marius and Paul, the Dubonnets came up with a formula consisting of wines from the Midi region, a dash of quinine, and to cover up its bitter taste, some of the spicy wine from the Greek island of Samos.

By the end of the century, Dubonnet was producing more than 3 million bottles a year, and exporting throughout the world.

Dubonnet went public in 1908, but the family retained managerial powers. There was a merger with the French branch of Cinzano in 1957, and later with Byrrh. In 1977, Pernod-Ricard acquired the company, and today the Dubonnet line is handled by Société Ricard.

The first Dubonnet poster, in 1894, featured one of Madame Dubonnet' cats. The following year, Chéret did his first QUINQUINA DUBONNET poster, and he continued the tradition; the girl in the green striped dress is a professional model, a charming soubrette from the Théâtre des Ambassadeurs named Lise Fleuron. The poster became so famous that Miss Fleuron was able to capitalize on it by billing herself thereafter as "The Girl with the Dubonnet Cat." And the cat, of course, was also held over by popular demand in next year's poster, with a different girl in a yellow dress.

5. ▶
Jules Chéret
QUINQUINA
DUBONNET
1896: Chaix, Paris
33⅞ x 49⅜ in./86 x 125.3 cm
Broido, 880
PAI-VIII, 145

QUINQUINA DUBONNET
APÉRITIF
dans tous les Cafés
IMPRIMERIE CHAIX (Ateliers Chéret), Rue Bergère, 20, PARIS — 21,166.96. (ENCRES LORILLEUX)

6.
Jules Chéret
BAL DU MOULIN
ROUGE
1889: Chaix, Paris
35 x 50½ in./89 x 128.2 cm
Broido, 316
Maindron, 257
Maitres, 53
DFP-II, 181
PAI-VIII, 38

The MOULIN ROUGE had just opened, and Chéret prepared its first two posters: one announcing the opening itself, which appears to be irretrievably lost, and this one for the remainder of the first season. The girls on the donkeys represent uninhibited fun at the new dance hall. Before long, customers would flock to the place not only to dance, but also to gape at the attraction that was to become symbolic of the whole era: the cancan, originally an English import based on the old-fashioned quadrille, which found its home here in a zestful version and thrilled an entire Victorian generation with its daring display of frilly feminine underthings. In fact, Chéret's poster for the Moulin Rouge season of the next year, 1890, already advertises what it calls "Paris-Cancan."

An interesting comparison may be made between this poster and one which was prepared for the Moulin Rouge by Toulouse-Lautrec (No. 40). Where Chéret depicts a pretty, idealized, airy scene which is pure esthetics, Toulouse-Lautrec goes for a strongly realistic rendering that is pure atmosphere, a down-to-earth feel of the place. Each artist attracts us to visit the establishment in his own way: Chéret appeals to our higher emotions, Toulouse-Lautrec to our baser instincts.

In the inset, we see Toulouse-Lautrec admiring Chéret's poster in an attitude of deep respect; he has even removed his hat. With him is Mr. Tremolada, assistant to the director of the Moulin Rouge.

7.
Jules Chéret
FOLIES-BERGERE/
FLEUR DE LOTUS
1893: Chaix, Paris
33⅛ x 47¼ in./84.1 x 120 cm
Broido, 126
Maindron, 114
PAI-IX, 208

The very name of the Folies-Bergère evokes the flavor of Paris in the Belle Epoque perhaps more vividly than any other single establishment. The Folies has been going strong since May Day of 1869 when it first opened its doors as a music hall, deriving its name from the nearby Rue Bergère. For a long time, it presented variety acts including boxing kangaroos and trapeze artists; its first revue worthy of the name, in which scads of more or less undraped girls became the chief attraction, did not arrive until 1886. By the turn of the century, the place was a major Paris landmark, and it retains its reputation to this day: hardly a visitor leaves Paris without seeing the most famous chorus line in the world at least once.

Chéret executed more than 60 posters for the Folies Bergère, between 1874, when the first major expansion of the business took place (there was an even bigger one in 1926), and 1897, the very zenith of its success. The names of the revues hardly matter, as all were meant mainly to present beautiful girls in attractive settings, and for FLEUR DE LOTUS, Chéret makes a spectacularly exuberant design, a masterpiece of graceful motion and pure joy.

a

b

c

d

e

f

The six color proofs plus final poster for the PANTOMIMES LUMINEUSES allows us a unique opportunity to see "inside" the lithographic process of Jules Chéret.

This is a modified version of what we today call "progressive color proofs." The first shows the red inking (a), followed by the yellow (b), and then the combination of the two (c). Then the blue is added (d), but we don't see how that came out in combination with the other colors. Chéret, however, did and he wanted more highlights and shadows and decided the best way to do that was to add an olive-green tint (e). The result is, in fact, the final state with letters (g). What is interesting is that the version "before letters" (f), was in fact a separate printing since the "drop-out" lettering of the show's title required an entirely separate blue stone. In addition to showing the great care and precision that went into the lithographic process, this also demonstrates the importance given to collectors of the period, as it was for them especially that these "avant lettres" (before letters) versions were so painstakingly run off.

8.
Jules Chéret
MUSEE GREVIN/
PANTOMIMES
LUMINEUSES
1892: Chaix, Pairs
34 x 48 in./86.4 x 121 cm
Broido, 468
Maindron, 381
DFP-II, 227
PAI-VIII, 54

g

Emile Reynaud (1844–1918), whose "Théâtre Optique" produced this show at the Musée Grévin, was a science teacher who combined a primitive peephole viewing apparatus with a projector, and came up with animated strips of celluloid pictures in color, coming as close to inventing movies as anyone could. He even used perforation to advance the images. After obtaining a patent in 1889, he put on his first public show at the Musée Grévin on October 28, 1892. Between then and 1900, there were 12,800 performances attended by more than 500,000 customers. However, Mr. Reynaud brooded over the fact that by then, regular motion pictures, perfected by others, left him in virtual obscurity. One day in 1900, he took all his apparatus and slides and tossed them into the river Seine. Eighteen years later, he died in a sanatorium, entirely forgotten by the world.

9.
Jules Chéret
MUSEE GREVIN / LES
DAMES HONGROISES
1888: Chaix, Paris
33¼ x 47⅛ in. / 84.5 x 119.6 cm
Broido, 465
Maindron, 378
PAI-IX, 202

MUSEE GREVIN was one of many museums of the late 19th century which discovered that their permanent exhibits were not enough to attract paying customers, and they offered various types of usually marginal entertainment as an added inducement. The Grevin specialized in artistic recreations of recent events of interest: in those days when news photography was in its infancy, many major events, from disasters to war battles, took place without being caught on film, and there were always enterpreneurs who tried to present them to the public in realistic, and often gory, presentations, using wax or papier-mâché figures and scenery in miniature, skillfully arranged so that perspective would give them depth.

Chéret prepared a number of posters for the Museum's special attractions, including magic shows, puppetry, the slide show of Professor Reynaud, and here LES DAMES HONGROISES, a Hungarian girls' orchestra.

10.
Jules Chéret
MUSEE GREVIN/
LES COULISSES
DE L'OPERA
1891: Chaix, Pairs
34¼ x 96 in./87 x 244 cm

Broido, 467
Maindron, 380
DFP-II, 210
Maitres, 37
PAI-VIII, 55

Hiatt called LES COULISSES DE L'OPERA "a delightfully piquant representation of a group of *premières danseuses* in the traditional costume" (p. 34), and it is indeed an outstanding achievement.

11.
Jules Chéret
LA BODINIERE
1900: Chaix, Paris
34⅛ x 48⅞ in./86.6 x 124 cm
Broido, 275
Maitres, 229
DFP-II, 266
PAI-VIII, 56

12.
Jules Chéret
LIDIA
1895: Chaix, Paris
33¾ x 48⅜ in./85.7 x 122.9 cm
Broido, 174
Maindron, 154
Maitres, 25
DFP-II, 250
PAI-IV, 140

LA BODINIERE was the exhibition hall of the Théâtre d'Application, offering a variety of attractions from art exhibits to shadow plays, one of which is being advertised here. It is evident that this was a stock poster whose bottom right quarter was left blank to insert the program of the week: in this case, probably, a second attraction was planned, but this specimen was pulled before its addition.

LIDIA was a headliner at some of the cabarets of Paris; this poster was meant for her appearance at the Alcazar d'Eté, and in the full version that text appears at top. The Alcazar had two locations: in the summer, on Champs-Elysée, in the winter at the Faubourg Poisonnière.

13
Jules Chéret
ELYSEE
MONTMARTRE
1890: Chaix, Paris
33¼ x 95⅞ in./84.5 x 243.5 cm
Broido, 320
Maindron, 260
DFP-II, 190
PAI-VIII, 120

The ELYSEE MONTMARTRE was a dance hall featuring a masked ball once a week, a standard custom of the epoch. Here, they also offer a "gala evening" on Wednesdays, giving you two chances to dress up in your fanciest duds.

Note how often Chéret uses yellow with his girls, giving them a sunny, cheerful personality.

Loie Fuller was a magic spectacle in turn-of-the-century Paris—a dancer with a unique act, simple in conception but dazzling in execution, in which she draped herself in yards of shimmering, gauzy fabric and swirled around on the stage illuminated by many-colored spotlights. The result was an iridescent phantasmagoria which fascinated Paris and the rest of Europe for years, made Miss Fuller a major celebrity, and created a whole school of dancing with emphasis on stunning visual effects.

The person behind the hullaballoo was a rather plain-looking Midwestern girl inclined to plumpness who had gone through the gamut of stock theatrics, vaudeville and cafe entertainment in her home country without much notice. Mary Louise Fuller was born in the Illinois town of Fullersburg, founded by one of her forefathers, in 1862. When she was still a child, the Fullers moved to Chicago where her father opened a family restaurant; since her mother had once been a singer, they encouraged the girl to perform for the patrons. By the age of 16, she was on the stage in New York, and for more than a decade acquired a variety of theatrical experience including straight acting, singing and dancing. It wasn't until 1891 that she discovered, by accident, what would remain her lasting career, when she had to perform a little dance in filmy veils in an obscure play "Quack, M.D." to suggest a hypnotic effect. The play faded quickly, but Mary Louise, by now already calling herself Loie, was fascinated by the interaction between lights and the material of her dress, and she set out to create her own specialty act.

Loie presented her new solo program for the first time on February 15, 1892 at the Casino in New York. It was received well enough for her to be able to ask for a raise and, failing to get it, accept a better offer from the rival Madison Square Theater where she remained for most of that spring. From the start, she wanted to try her act out in Paris, the artists' Mecca of the 1890's, and after being forced to accept a detour through Germany, finally made it to the Folies-Bergère, where she opened on November 5, 1892.

The rest is history. Within days, it was necessary to make advance reservations to get into the Folies-Bergère at all; at the end of two months, there was an imitator doing a similar act in London and at least three others in smaller cabarets of Paris; the Folies-Bergère held an unprecedented matinee performance so women and children could see the fascinating spectacle; and Paris shops were flooded with Loie Fuller merchandise—all unmistakable signs of a major hit.

Not surprisingly, for the rest of her life Loie lived in Europe, taking her act around, devising ever more spectacular special effects, and from 1908 on running her own school for aspiring dancers. In the process, she made many friends among artists, intellectuals and royalty; strangely, despite many offers, she was married only once, briefly, and that was in the United States before her success; evidently, the experience left her wary of another total commitment. She died in 1928, but not before her coterie of ardent admirers immortalized her in paintings, portraits, sculpture, limited-edition prints and photographs. They wrote odes and poems for her, dedicated their books to her, and made her one of the most celebrated American expatriates of her era.

To capture her brilliant art on canvas or paper was a challenge to any artist. Her dance was constant movement and sparkle, which no still photograph could do justice to, and the ever-changing dazzle of colors taxed any painter's palette. Fellow American James McNeill Whistler tried to capture her elusive magic, as did Georges Lemmen, Marie-Felix Lucas, Charles Maurin and others. Henri de Toulouse-Lautrec made a series of 50 lithographs to show the endless color combinations of her act.

The best posterists of the era vied to prepare lithographs worthy of her splendor. Bac had the honor of publicizing her debut in 1892; he was followed by Chéret, Orazi, Pal, Georges Meunier, deFeure, Choubrac, Leymarie…

Chéret was a natural choice to depict her, as movement and elan were rampant in much of his best work. He addressed the subject in three posters—the FOLIES-BERGERE/LA LOIE FULLER of 1893 shown here, and two in 1897—and painted a pastel portrait of her, of unknown date, apparently not connected to any poster. In all instances, he achieved spectacular results with swirling lines and splashes of color, catching the essence of a belle epoque phenomenon.

14.
Jules Chéret
FOLIES-BERGERE
LA LOIE FULLER
1893: Chaix, Paris
33⅞ x 48 in./85.7 x 121.8 cm
Broido, 125
Maindron, 113
DFP-II, 233
PAI-IX, 207

15.
Jules Chéret
LA LANTERNE/
P'TIT MI
1888: Chaix, Paris
34½ x 48⅝ in./87.7 x 123.5 cm
Broido, 659
Maindron, 546
DFP-II, 175
PAI-IX, 203

16.
Jules Chéret
LE COURRIER
FRANCAIS
1891: Chaix, Paris
34¾ x 48¾ in./88.3 x 123.8 cm
Broido, 580
Maindron, 470
Maitres, 49
PAI-IX, 224

Two Paris dailies make use of Chéret's charming designs.

A universal custom of the day was for periodicals to publish popular novels in installments, to assure themselves of continuing interest by the fickle public; here, LA LANTERNE launches a romantic tale, "P'tit Mi".

The design for the COURRIER FRANCAIS was used in several ways: originally, it advertised two different art exhibits sponsored by the paper; here, with all the text other than the paper's name removed, it served as a poster to solicit readership; and finally, various editions, some on high-quality paper, were sold to poster art collectors.

18.
Jules Chéret
BONNARD-BIDAULT
1887: Chaix, Paris
35 x 48½ in./88.8 x 125.7 cm
Broido, 1045
Maindron, 864
PAI-IX, 199

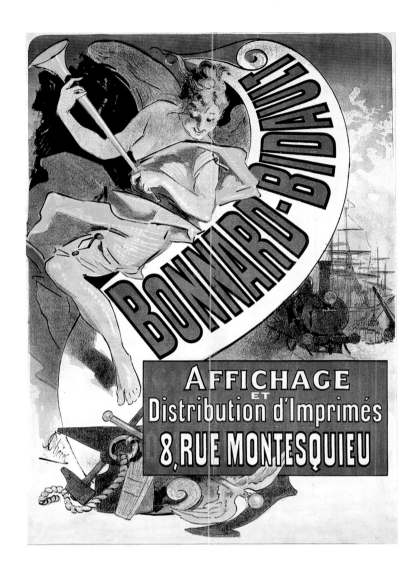

17.
Jules Chéret
HALLE AUX
CHAPEAUX
1892: Chaix, Paris
33¾ x 48¾ in./85.8 x 123.9 cm
Broido, 830
Maindron, 704
PAI-VIII, 82

In his work for commercial clients, Chéret stayed with his fabulous damsels, sometimes showing them as satisfied consumers. In the HALLE AUX CHAPEAUX design, it's the little girl imitating her mother that gives it a special warmth. For BONNARD-BIDAULT, a poster distributing firm, Chéret solves the problem of showing a pretty girl by making her an allegorical figure representing the industry.

19.
Jules Chéret
PALAIS DE GLACE
1896: Chaix, Paris
33⅞ x 48¼ in./86 x 122.5 cm

Broido, 369
Maitres, 17
DFP-II, 256
Schardt, p. 50–51
PAI-VIII, 111

For the PALAIS DE GLACE, Chéret executed some half dozen designs, most of which were printed in different sizes: in each, a pretty skater is the focus, generally with one or more attentive gentlemen hovering discreetly around to assist her if she should stumble.

20.
Jules Chéret
SAXOLEINE
1900: Chaix, Paris
33¾ x 48⅛ in./85.8 x 122.1 cm
Broido, 957
DFP-II, 209
PAI-VIII, 85

The SAXOLEINE series—ten posters executed over an 11-year period—is virtually a textbook on how to use feminine allure to advertise a mundane product, here a brand of kerosene for home lighting and heating. All of them show a young and pretty homemaker, carefully groomed and dressed, either lighting a lamp or, as in this case, warming herself by a heater; and in every design, the background, without showing any details, consists of tones of red, orange or yellow which suggest a homey, friendly atmosphere.

21.
Jules Chéret
JOB
1895: Chaix, Paris
34¼ x 47½ in./87 x 120.5 cm
Broido, 1028
Maindron, 850
Maitres, 1
DFP-II, 255
Weill, 35
PAI-VIII, 98

   JOB was a cigarette paper; here, Chéret's aim was to hint subtly that "rolling your own" need not necessarily be purely a man's thing. Clearly, though, it would have required, in the Victorian era, a girl of some spunk to invade such a male prerogative, and so Chéret gives her an appropriately defiant, headstrong mien, with loud red hair for extra emphasis. The master at his masterly best.

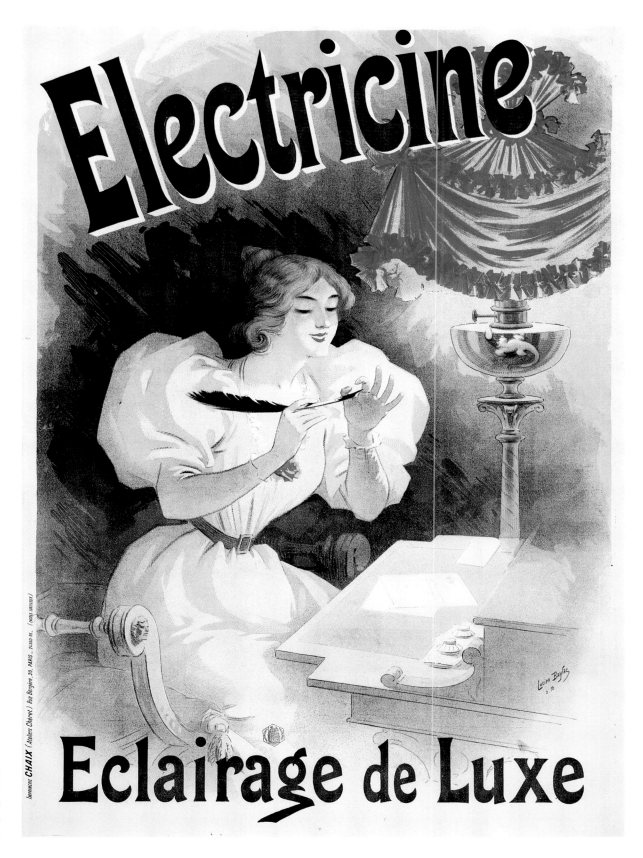

22.
Lucien Baylac
ELECTRICINE
1895: Chaix, Paris
34 x 48 in./86.4 x 122 cm
DFP-II, 54

Lucien Baylac

Lucien Baylac is a bit of an enigma, known to us solely from ten posters produced in a one-year period 1894—95. That he is a disciple of Chéret is self-evident; everything else about his life and other artistic endeavors, if any, is a mystery.

ELECTRICINE was an ordinary lamp kerosene whose manufacturer wanted to make use of the awe in which electricity was held at the time by naming its product after it, and claiming it gave light every bit as bright. The point is made by showing the girl getting ready to write a letter under its illumination.

23.
Alfred Choubrac
AUX TRAVAILLEURS
Ca. 1890: F. Appel, Paris
38¼ x 58¾ in. / 100.6 x 141.6 cm

24. ▶
Alfred Choubrac
FOLIES-BERGERE/
ARMAND ARY
Ca. 1894: F. Appel, Paris
32¾ x 47¼ in. / 83.2 x 120.7 cm
Maindron, p. 52
Reims, 545

Alfred Choubrac

Alfred Choubrac (1853–1902) was one of the handful of posterists who gained prominence before the Golden Nineties. Educated in classic art at the Ecole des Beaux-Arts in his native Paris, he started out as a painter of military scenes in collaboration with his brother Leon. To make a living, he did caricatures and illustrations for *Gil Blas, L'Echo de Paris, Le Courrier Français* and some other papers; later, he became a scene designer for theaters at which he was very successful. In the early 1880s, Choubrac joined the fledgling group of poster designers: in 1884, when Maindron published the first article on the subject, he listed only nine active posterists known to him, and in the first poster exhibition, held that same year in the Passage Vivienne in Paris, only three of them were represented: Chéret and the two Choubrac brothers.

AUX TRAVAILLEURS is an example of a purely informative poster for a clothing store from the mid-1880s. Nevertheless, Choubrac makes an attempt to give the scene a lift beyond mere manikins: note for example the little girl's adoring look at her mother.

The FOLIES-BERGERE poster of a few years later, however, already unmistakably exudes the aura of the 90s, with the flowery decoration and elaborate lettering. An unusual feature is the way the singer is shown both in full figure and as a portrait—perhaps a bit of narcissism on the part of the performer, who apparently borrowed at least one stage style, the wearing of long black gloves, from the celebrated Yvette Guilbert.

25.
Georges Meunier
LOX
1895: Chaix, Paris
32 x 45⅜ in./81.3 x 115.2 cm
DFP-II, 586
Meunier, 22
Maindron, p. 91
Reims, 865
PAI-IX, 353

26. ▶
Georges Meunier
OTARD DUPUY & CO.
COGNAC
Ca. 1896: Chaix, Paris
33⅞ x 48½ in./86 x 123.2 cm

Georges Meunier

Georges Meunier (1869–1942), a native of Paris, was educated both in the classical tradition and in the new decorative arts. He started as a painter, good enough to have works accepted for exhibition by the Société des Artistes Français as well as the Salon des Humoristes. In poster work, in which he became active at the age of 25, he was greatly influenced by Chéret; in fact, much of his work was lithographed at the Chaix shop where Chéret also did his posters. A majority of Georges Meunier's poster output dates from the Golden Years, 1894–98; later, he became more active as a book illustrator.

Both posters show a sense of humor: the LOX scene is played strictly for laughs, with the guzzling girl cyclist and her companion with a ludicrous mustache, while the OTARD DUPUY poster virtually duplicates the idea on a higher and more subtle level; obviously, whether low class or high society, the gentlemen can barely conceal their eager anticipation of the drink taking its effect on the ladies.

OTARD DUPUY & Cº
COGNAC

27.
Georges Meunier
JARDIN DE PARIS /
MONTAGNES RUSSES
NAUTIQUES
1895: Chaix, Paris
34⅝ x 48¾ in./88 x 123.9 cm .
Meunier, 20
Reims, 863
PAI-V, 227

MONTAGNES RUSSES is an early French term for the first timid roller coasters, and a "nautical" version thereof would today be obviously just a water slide—but, as the illustration makes clear, a fairly elaborate one, no doubt the high point of a trip to the Garden of Paris. But just in case the reference to Russian mountains isn't enough, there's also a hint of the American Niagara Falls—the Garden's publicist wasn't overlooking any angle.

28.
René Péan
MERS-LES-BAINS
Ca. 1900: Chaix, Paris
33¼ x 47¼ in./84.2 x 120 cm

René Péan

René Péan (1875–?) worked with Chéret's printer, Chaix, in the period 1890–1905, and was one of the Master's most brilliant followers. Most of his work was done for various theaters and cabarets, as well as some very early films; he was also actively involved in poster work for the Paris World's Fair of 1900.

The travel poster for the MERS-LES-BAINS resort on the Channel coast is therefore something of an exception for Péan, but he acquits himself nobly, focusing our attention on an endearing little scene at the beach.

29.
Misti
FETE DE NEUILLY
1905: Lithographie Nouvelle,
Asnières
37¼ x 54¼ in. / 99.7 x 137.9 cm

Misti

Misti was the pseudonym for Ferdinand Mifliez (1865–1923), painter and lithographer born in Paris. His paintings were shown in the salons of the Société des Artistes Français as well as the Humorists. In the period 1894–1914, he was one of the busiest posterists, doing much work for one of the city's major department stores (Magasin de Pygmalion) and for the Dubonnet company.

He settled permanently in Neuilly, and produced several posters for the town's annual 3-week festivals. This FETE DE NEUILLY is one of the most charming versions: two sweet young ladies with sunflowers and an avid pursuer who is trying to make up his mind which one of them might be more likely to succumb to his monocled handsomeness.

THE CLASSICISTS

Like all artists, poster designers may be categorized according to various criteria, but such designations should never be taken or intended as an attempt to place anyone in a definitive pigeonhole. Rather, such purely arbitrary classifications are used in most cases, and certainly in this book, as a device to help create some measure of order out of an infinite variety of artistic expressions.

In this instance, we thought it might be helpful to arrange the artists according to the thematic and stylistic approach they most often apply. The Classicist may be defined as an artist who came to posters only after a thorough grounding in traditional painting techniques, who derives his inspiration from legend, mythology, religion or medieval styles, and whose posters exude a pristine austerity without regard for commercial or popular excesses of the times.

It bears repeating that while there may be limits to art there is no limit to any individual artist, and our arbitrary divisions are not meant to stick a label on anybody.

Eugène Grasset

Eugène Grasset (1845–1917) was born in Lausanne, Switzerland and studied architecture in Zurich. He even started working for an architect, but in 1871 moved to Paris and embarked on a career in art. He dabbled in all aspects of it: metal, ceramics, furniture design, windows, jewelry, tapestry. In 1877, he became interested in color lithography and illustrative techniques, and again went for a whole gamut of the subject: magazine covers, decorative panels, book illustration, cards, postage stamps, typography, book design. On the side, he entered a contest for the design of a fountain, did a mosaic for a church, and designed the interior of the Chat Noir cabaret. In posters, he affects a formalistic, classic approach, often with something of a medieval symbolism faintly present.

Grasset was an apostle of the decorative trend in art, and is often credited with giving a major impetus to the style which was eventually called *art nouveau*. His creed was the democratization of art in all its expressions, and to this end he worked tirelessly, teaching (and, in the view of some, preaching) his conviction to everyone he could reach. He taught decorative painting at the Ecole Guerin, and wrote several authoritative books which belong among the bibles of art nouveau: "La Plante et ses Applications Ornementales" (1898–9) and "La Méthode de Composition Ornementale" (1905) are two of the most important ones. He even had a type face he designed named after him.

30.
Eugène Grasset
ABRICOTINE
1905: Devambez, Paris
39⅞ x 29¼ in./101.4 x 74.2
DFP-II, 420
PAI-IV, 178

In ABRICOTINE, Grasset doesn't show the product but suggests its origin by depicting a comely young apricot picker.

31.
Eugène Grasset
LIBRAIRIE
ROMANTIQUE
1887: J. Bognard, Paris
33¾ x 50⅛ in./85.7 x 127.3 in.
Arwas, p. 32
Maindron, p. 129
Maitres, 42
DFP-II, 398
PAI-III, 302

LIBRAIRIE ROMANTIQUE was a series of novels published by the Monnier firm in Paris. This was a stock poster for the whole series, with names of individual volumes placed in the blank space as they were issued (see inset). Appropriately, Grasset used a style associated with the age of romanticism—the girl in velvet and lace, a cathedral which is a perfect setting for a romantic novel.

32.
Eugène Grasset
MASSON/CHOCOLAT
MEXICAIN
1897: G. de Malherbe, Paris
18¼ x 25⅛ in./46.4 x 64 cm
Arwas, p. 37
DFP-II, 416
PAI-VII, 160

Two more facets of the versatile Grasset: for MASSON, he frames a warm home scene in a rigorous geometric pattern, and in the stock poster for the ODEON, he carefully composes a view of the loge section of the theater. Posters have been found with text containing details of programs from the 1890–91 season (see top inset).

The ODEON design is a particularly charming composition, a graceful young lady in a gown that is quite modern by contemporary standards, accompanied by a matron in a far more conservative dress, looking every bit like the proper chaperone. The effect is so good, and its realization as a lithograph so successful, that the publisher and printer, G. de Malherbe and H. A. Cellot, later used this design to advertise their firm's printing skills—simply by replacing the theater text with new advertising copy (see bottom inset).

33.
Eugène Grasset
L'ODÉON
1890: G. de Malherbe, Paris
32⅝ x 47⅞ in./83 x 121.6 cm
DFP-II, 400
PAI-VI, 111

Paul Berthon

Paul Berthon (1872–1909) studied painting and sculpture in his native town of Villefranche, then transferred to the School of Decorative Arts in Paris. He was greatly influenced by Grasset, and like him became a jack-of-all-trades: he designed book bindings, dabbled in ceramics, furniture, and illustrated books. In 1895 he became attracted to lithography and started producing posters; eventually, he joined the art department of a railroad, Chemins de Fer de l'Ouest.

In his posters and decorative panels, of which he designed a prodigious number, he adopted much of the stiff formalism of Grasset but gave it a softer, almost pious dimension, in dreamily gentle shades of pastel colors. His last poster, for a film, was printed in 1910, after his death.

Even in his relatively brief life span (he died when he was only 37), Berthon produced a body of work shining with genteel beauty. In an interview for the British magazine *The Poster*, he gave the following account, somewhat awkwardly stated (but that may be the fault of the translator), of his technique:

"As a rule I draw direct on the stone, after having massed my general effect in colours on a rough sketch. Then I take a first print in the tint of the outline; then accordingly I keep to the second colour or alter it, and on the second proof I try to find the effects of the following colours and so forth. Very often I modify entirely my first conception of a design, but in return I obtain the effects I want, and working on the stone myself, I am able to rule everything as I want it." (May 1899, p. 205).

34.
Paul Berthon
SOURCE DES ROCHES
1899: Chaix, Paris
19¼ x 16⅛ in./48.9 x 41 cm
Arwas, p. 99

35. ▶
Paul Berthon
LE LIVRE DE MAGDA
1898: Chaix, Paris
19 x 25⅛ in./48.2 x 63.8 cm
Arwas, p. 97
DFP-II, 66
PAI-VII, 45

SOURCE DES ROCHES uses a subdued palette in the service of a mundane product, but there is no compomise with Berthon's artistic sensitivity; he alone can deliver a plain commercial message as if it were a sermon.

LE LIVRE DE MAGDA, a poster advertising a collection of poetry by Armand Silvestre, shows the strange ethereal sensuality which can be found in much of Berthon's work: never blatantly sexy, his women radiate a soft, yielding glow that gives them a spiritual beauty. Note how a perfectly harmonious effect is created with only a few shades of muted yellows and browns.

36.
Paul Berthon
SALON DES 100
1895: A. Davy, Paris
17⅛ x 22 in./43.5 x 50.7 cm

Arwas, p. 94
DFP-II, 61
Weill, 53
Reims, 231
PAI-VII, 375c

SALON DES CENT was a permanent exhibition hall maintained by the magazine *La Plume* on its premises to display posters that were on sale through its marketing department, Affiches d'Art. Nearly every posterist of note was asked at one time or another to prepare a poster for an exhibit there, and this is Berthon's entry, before the addition of text (see inset). Again, it's character that Berthon depicts, rather than prettiness.

The unusual theme of the blonde performer against a spider web can be explained by the fact that LIANE DE POUGY was appearing in a skit titled "The Golden Spider" at the Folies-Bergère in October of 1896. She was born Anne-Marie Chasseigne, a strikingly beautiful girl whose early marriage ended disastrously when her husband shot her in a jealous fit. After recovery, she changed her name, entered show business, and became a famous seductress whose conquests were legion—generally the wealthiest patrons of the arts, including the then Prince of Wales, according to persistent rumors; in 1910, she actually married a prince. Strangely, that marriage lasted quite happily and peacefully for 30 years until his death; she then spent the last few years of her life in a convent.

Interestingly, LIANE DE POUGY is the only Berthon design that works strictly as a poster; everything else he did has a painterly feeling and is most effective as art for the home.

37. ▶
Paul Berthon
FOLIES BERGERE/
LIANE DE POUGY
1896: Lemercier, Paris
24½ x 61⅛ in./62.2 x 155.2 cm

DFP-II, 63
Reims, 230
Folies-Bèrgere, 24

38.
Maurice Réalier-Dumas
CHAMPAGNE JULES
MUMM & CO.
1895: Chaix, Paris
12 x 34½ in./30.5 x 87.6 cm
DFP-II, 733
Maitres, 111
Boissons, 16

39.
Maurice Réalier-Dumas
EXPOSITION/
GALERIE G. PETIT
1895: V. Palyart, Paris
22¾ x 70½ in./57.2 x 179.1 cm
DFP-II, 734
Reims, 979
PAI-II, 209

Maurice Réalier-Dumas

Maurice Réalier-Dumas (1860–1928) was a native Parisian who attended the Ecole Nationale de Beaux-Arts and became a competent painter, in a style that was in the academic mainstream at his time. He had no difficulty gaining admission to the Société des Artistes Francais, where he exhibited his paintings uninterruptedly for more than 40 years starting in 1886. In his poster work, which is rather infrequent and rare, he adopted however a wholly different technique, of simple lines, flat colors, and economy of design. Maindron said of him that he seems to derive his inspiration from Greek vases; and indeed, both works shown here— CHAMPAGNE MUMM and EXPOSITION/GALERIE PETIT—manifest a certain classic austerity that could well be so described.

It was a German family with vineyards in the Rhine Valley that established a wine business at Reims in 1827. Gottlieb de Mumm, with a partner named Giesler, started operating as Mumm Giesler & Cie; but in 1838, Gottlieb's son Georg Hermann changed it to G. H. Mumm, a name which by then began to be associated with quality champagne—especially the world famous Cordon Rouge. A second branch of the family set up a new firm, Jules Mumm & Co., in 1852; it went into receivership in 1910 and G. H. Mumm took it over. Accepted from the start at the Court of Weimar, and later also at those of England and Spain, Mumm became known as "the champagne of sovereigns." The company remains in business to this day, having been acquired by Seagram's.

HENRI de TOULOUSE-LAUTREC

Self-appointed purists and academicians have always maintained that applied art is sullied art, or no art at all, and that artists who are willing to apply their talents to commercial subjects are somehow inferior as artists. But then came Toulouse-Lautrec—and the distinction became, shall we say, academic. For here was an acknowledged master who, suddenly and unexpectedly, turned his attention to the humble poster, and effortlessly proved that the quality of his artistry didn't suffer at all in the transition.

HENRI DE TOULOUSE-LAUTREC

Henri de Toulouse-Lautrec (1864–1901) came from an aristocratic background, having been born the son of an earl. Even as a schoolboy he showed a talent for drawing, covering every paper and book margin with subjects he knew, mainly farm animals, horses and riders. At 14, his family arranged for him to take lessons from animal painter René Princeteau in Paris. By this time, already, he had suffered two riding accidents which eventually left him crippled for life.

Photo: Roger-Viollet, Paris

At the age of 18, he made the final decision to stay in Paris and study art seriously. He found lodgings in Montmartre and mingled with its denizens, honing his craft among like-minded contemporaries; among them were Léon Bonnat, Fernand Cormon, Louis Anquentin, Emile Bernard, as well as Dégas and Van Gogh. He became a frequenter of the cafés, cabarets and brothels of the neighborhood, drawing from them inspirations for his artistic themes. Among his early patrons was Aristide Bruant, a rough-hewn entertainer who owned the Mirliton, one of Toulouse-Lautrec's favorite haunts; Bruant exhibited his work, published some of it in his magazine (also called *Le Mirliton*), and later gave him poster assignments. As the artist's stature grew, he found other magazines eager to publish his work, among them *La Revue Blanche, L'Escarmouche* and *Le Rire*. His subjects continued to be the types he came in contact during his rounds: many of them anonymous loafers, street girls, vendors and the like, but also some of the famous music-hall artists who became his friends, such as the singer Yvette Guilbert, cancan dancers Jane Avril and La Goulue, stage stars May Milton, Yahne, May Belfort and many others. In 1896, he published a collection of lithographs, "Elles," with scenes from the local brothels. He became absorbed in the night life of Montmartre until he himself was an indispensable part of it.

From the beginning, his drawings showed an unerring eye for catching facial characteristics, expressions and mannerisms with deadly accuracy and yet with the most sparing means, a few lines, a carefully chosen perspective, or an imperceptible emphasis that focuses our attention.

In 1891, Toulouse-Lautrec was greatly impressed with Pierre Bonnard's FRANCE-CHAM-PAGNE poster (No.57), and decided to investigate the potential of lithography. Working with Bonnard's lithographer Ancourt, he learned the craft from the bottom up—and within months, brought it to an unprecedented artistic zenith. He managed to cram some 400 litho-graphs into the remaining ten years of his life, 31 of which were posters, and all of which were the cream of graphic design. His masterpieces define the limits of poster style: where Chéret epitomizes a completely external, impersonal viewpoint, Toulouse-Lautrec is the embodiment of internal, personal vision with a point to make—not, to be sure, a moral judgment, but rather an amused, wry observation on the passing scene.

Virtually all posterists, then and since, have had to make their stance somewhere between these two poles. True, some may have tried a satirical bite more vicious than Toulouse-Laut-rec's, or a neutrality even more profound than Chéret's, but none could surpass the sheer mas-tery of the pioneers. The best proof is that a century later, their work still sparkles with all its force, inventiveness and beauty, and each in his way is more popular than they ever were in their own lifetimes.

Toulouse-Lautrec's fame grew steadily during the 90s, and his works were exhibited in gal-leries throughout Europe; often he traveled to other countries to accompany the exhibit. How-ever, the years of night life and the excessive intake of absinthe began to take their toll, and his physical condition became very fragile. He had to be taken through the Paris World's Fair of 1900 in a wheel-chair, and the following year he died in his country home.

His legacy in poster art continues to astound us. Despite the smallness of his output, as com-pared with the rest of his artistic oeuvre, Toulouse-Lautrec proved himself to be a true genius of the poster, and his position in the poster pantheon has never been seriously challenged.

When Toulouse-Lautrec started learning the art of lithoghraphy, he mentioned it to Charles Zidler, the director of the Moulin Rouge, who immediately offered to let him prepare a new poster for the cabaret, to replace the ones by Chéret which had been in use for two years (No. 6). The artist rose to the occasion—with the result that the first poster as well as the first lithograph he ever made turned out to be also his biggest, best and most successful. It extended his already considerable fame beyond the confines of the art circles to the broadest cross section of the public, and made him an instant popular celebrity.

The MOULIN ROUGE is, indeed, a masterpiece in every respect: it not only catches the essential characteristics of its two subjects, La Goulue the dancer (Louise Weber) and Valentin le Désossé, her partner (Etienne Renaudin), but it also instantly explains the very heart of the cancan: the dazzle of the petticoats, which Toulouse-Lautrec creates simply by leaving the paper blank. Nothing could be more direct or more illuminating: the artist gets his point across with an impact no passer-by can resist. In his first lesson, Toulouse-Lautrec grasps the quintessence of poster language: catch attention, speak forcefully, deliver the message.

The MOULIN ROUGE poster is also a rare example of an early recognition of an artwork's value. Only five years later, one of the first catalogues of posters for sale, from the dealer Arnould, which lists most of the Chérets and the other Toulouse-Lautrec designs then available in the 3-to-5 franc range, lists this one without even the top third banner at the outrageous price of 25 francs. One can almost hear many a patron grumbling that no poster is worth such a fortune...

As far as the poster collecting community knows, no more than half a dozen copies of a good condition, three-sheet version remain in private hands, and their value has been rising at a remarkable rate: in fact, at the moment, this is the most highly prized single poster ever sold at a public auction, fetching $220,000 in 1989.

40.
Henri de
Toulouse-Lautrec
MOULIN ROUGE
1891: Ch. Levy, Paris
48½ x 77½ in./123.2 x 196.8 cm
Delteil, 339
Adhemar, 1
Wittrock, P1B
Adriani, 1-II
DFP-II, 822
Weill, 46
Maitres, 122
PAI-VIII, 521

In 1892, Toulouse-Lautrec made the acquaintance of the dancer Jane Avril and made several sketches and paintings of her. They became close friends, and eventually he immortalized her in four posters: two of them with her alone, one in which she performs in a quartet known as the Troupe of Mademoiselle Eglantine, and one where she is a patron of the Divan Japonais accompanied by critic Edouard Dujardin.

In his first poster, he shows JANE AVRIL on stage doing her specialty, which, according to contemporaries, was essentially a cancan that she made extra exotic by making a pretense of prudery—the "depraved virgin" image aimed at arousing the prurience in the predominantly male audience. The sexual innuendo was captured by the artist by contrasting the dancer's slender legs with the robust, phallic neck of the bass viol in the foreground—a masterly stroke that not only heightens our perception but also creates an unusual perspective: we see the performer as an orchestra member would, and this allows Toulouse-Lautrec to show, as if inadvertently, how tired and somehow downcast she looks from close-up, not at all in keeping with the gaiety of the dance that is perceived by the audience. It is clear, as Maindron has pointed out, that she is dancing entirely for the viewer's pleasure, not hers, which makes it a highly poignant image. Seemingly without trying, Toulouse-Lautrec not only creates a great poster but makes a personal statement: only a sensitive person who really cares about his subject as a human being would portray her with such startling candor.

41.
Henri de
Toulouse-Lautrec
JANE AVRIL
1893: Chaix, Paris
36 x 49⅜ in./91.5 x 125.4 cm
Delteil, 345
Adhemar, 12
Wittrock, P6B
Adriani, 11-I
DFP-II, 828
Maitres, 110
PAI-VII, 328

A much more composed Jane Avril is seen in the DIVAN JAPONAIS poster, where she is just a patron watching the show—but the same bass viol looks at her, now from the opposite angle, and it appears to be almost smiling, as if the whole thing were an inside joke. Jane is accompanied—or, more likely, being accosted—by noted critic Edouard Dujardin, no doubt with amorous intentions, but her faintly bemused expression indicates that she is used to this, and will be able to handle him without any trouble.

Note that the performer—although it is a great celebrity, the famous Yvette Guilbert—is not the focus of the poster, and Toulouse-Lautrec makes sure of it not only by placing her somewhat indistinctly in the poorly-lit background, but even by going to the length of deliberately cutting her head off. It's not that he had anything against her; on the contrary, they were friends, and he portrayed her frequently. But on this occasion, he wanted to turn our attention to the clientele of this small intimate cabaret rather than to its performers.

The Divan prided itself on catering to the literati and the intelligentsia of the day: it was decorated in Japanese style, with paper lanterns and fake bamboo, at a time when Oriental prints and artifacts were the latest rage among art connoisseurs, and it hoped thereby to attract the trend setters. The poster was prepared at the request of Edouard Fournier, manager of the Divan Japonais, who took over the reins of the *café-concert* from its founder, Jehan Sarrazin, in the fall of 1892.

In both posters, Toulouse-Lautrec has made good use of spatter, a technique which adds another dimension to poster art: here, for example, it effectively separates the solid black of Jane's dress from the less important dark mass of the bar and the orchestra. Spatter can also add depth and three-dimensionality, and Toulouse-Lautrec was to use it in much of his lithograhic work; yet, surprisingly enough, it is rarely if ever employed by other posterists, perhaps because of the sheer technical difficulty of it. But he, having acquired the skills of a lithographer, could work right alongside the printing plant employees and achieve whatever effect he desired.

42.
Henri de
Toulouse-Lautrec
DIVAN JAPONAIS
1893: Edw. Ancourt, Paris
25½ x 33 in. / 64.9 x 83.9 cm

Delteil, 341
Adhemar, 11
Wittrock, P11
Adriani, 8
Maitres, 2
DFP-II, 824
PAI-VII, 331

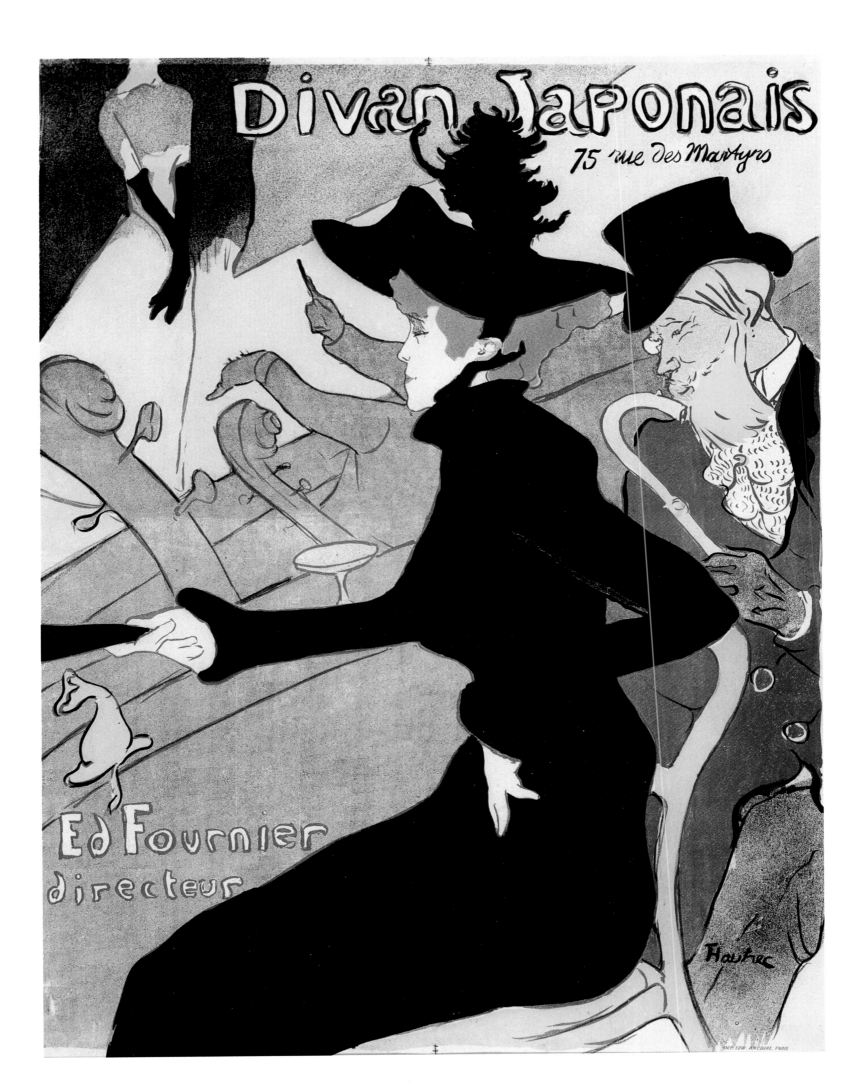

43.
Henri de
Toulouse-Lautrec
TROUPE DE MLLE
EGLANTINE
1896
30¾ x 23 in./78.2 x 58.4 cm

Delteil, 361
Adhemar, 198
Wittrock, P21C
Adriani, 162-III
DFP-II, 850
PAI-IX, 520

At the height of cancan's popularity, dancers formed groups which offered their services as a unit; whether the TROUPE DE MLLE EGLANTINE was the best of them we don't know, but it is certainly the only one publicized by the best. Toulouse-Lautrec did it at the request of his friend Jane Avril. From left to right, we see Jane Avril, Cléopâtra, Eglantine and Gazelle. As with his MOULIN ROUGE poster, he lets the white of the petticoats, punctuated by stockinged legs, do most of the talking, but he also offhandedly gives each girl a distinct character in only a few lines limning their facial expressions.

Toulouse-Lautrec's last poster for JANE AVRIL was also one of the last he ever made, as shortly after he completed it he entered a sanatorium for the first of several recuperative stays. In the art nouveau period, the snake is an image fraught with symbolism, and it may have been meant to suggest that Jane was being stifled as an artist—perhaps by her own passions, perhaps by "the art of her time," as Abdy would have it, perhaps simply by ravages of time. Whatever the symbolism, it is something of a departure for the artist, with only the performer's image on white background, unlike any other poster he ever did.

The unwonted starkness of the poster may have discouraged Jane's impressario, for according to Abdy he didn't like it, despite the performer's personal approval, and did not permit it to be used for publicity purposes.

44. ▶
Henri de
Toulouse-Lautrec
JANE AVRIL
1899: H. Stern, Paris
14½ x 21⅝ in./36.9 x 55 cm

Delteil, 367
Adhemar, 323
Wittrock, P29B
Adriani, 354-II
DFP-II, 851
PAI-IV, 273

JANE
Avril

H.Stern, Paris.

1899

45.
Henri de
Toulouse-Lautrec
MAY MILTON
1895
23⅝ x 30⅞ in. / 60 x 78.5 cm

Delteil, 336
Adhemar, 149
Wittrock, P17B
Adriani, 134-II
DFP-II, 836
PAI-VII, 337

MAY MILTON was another performer befriended by Toulouse-Lautrec; apparently she was not a major headliner, as precious little information is available on her, and we may assume that the poster was a personal favor. It was allegedly prepared for an American tour for her which never materialized. She was an English girl, and as Toulouse-Lautrec somewhat unmercifully shows, neither facial beauty nor taste in clothes were among her strong suits: her face could sink a fleet of ships, and her dress is a shapeless sack. There being no record of a girl trying to scratch Toulouse-Lautrec's eyes out, we must assume she was able to take it, knowing there was no personal malice in him.

The Montmartre chansonnier turned restaurateur, ARISTIDE BRUANT, was a strong, imposing personality, and in the several posters of him Toulouse-Lautrec conveys this by letting him dominate the picture completely, with virtually nothing else to distract our attention, and with Bruant's characteristic red scarf, hat and walking stick adding impact to the image. Bruant was from the start a staunch supporter of the newcomer; arrogant he may have been, but he could certainly recognize talent when he saw it, and made no bones about encouraging it. It is stated by Edouard Julien that this design, for example, was immediately seen by Bruant as a masterpiece, but the manager of the Ambassadeurs rejected it as too brutally frank and unflattering; the only way the performer could get it accepted was "by warning the manager that he would not appear on the stage unless there was a copy of the poster on either side of the proscenium, and unless the whole of Paris was plastered with further copies." (Julien, p.16.) The singer also used the poster, with the image reversed, to advertise his appearance at the Eldorado, but using a different printer.

46. ▶
Henri de
Toulouse-Lautrec
AMBASSADEURS /
ARISTIDE BRUANT
1892: Edw. Ancourt, Paris
37⅞ x 56⅞ in. / 96.2 x 144.5 cm

Delteil, 343
Adhemar, 6
Wittrock, P4
Adriani, 3
DFP-II, 825
PAI-IX, 515

AMBASSADEURS
aristide
BRUANT
dans
son cabaret
HLautrec
IMP. EDW. ANCOURT & Cie 83, Fg St DENIS

47.
Henri de
Toulouse-Lautrec
LE DEUXIÈME
VOLUME DE BRUANT
1893: Chaix, Paris
23¾ x 31½ in./60.3 x 90 cm
Delteil, 349
Adhemar, 71
Wittrock, P10C
Adriani, 57
PAI-IX, 522

From all accounts, Bruant was forceful, brutally honest, in many ways a highly abrasive personality who spoke in the coarse vernacular of the streets and was not above showing his contempt for patrons who displeased him or making vulgar remarks about them. But he was also brimming with talent, enterprise and shrewd business acumen, making him one of the most formidable figures of the day.

Toulouse-Lautrec catches the showman's disdain graphically by having him give us the broad of his back; in the one case, totally, in the other, adding a sneer over his shoulder, with the red scarf making the exclamation point. As noted before, Bruant had no trouble dealing with his friend's less-than-complimentary portraits: he loved all three of them and made multiple use of them as posters with different texts.

The image with the hands stuck resolutely in his pockets was used, in its first application, to advertise Bruant's performances at his own cabaret, Le Mirliton; next, it announced the opening of his new venture, Théâtre Aristide Bruant; and finally, here, it advertises LE DEUXIEME VOLUME DE BRUANT, the publication of the second volume of his songs in book form, with illustrations by Steinlen.

The haughty Bruant in LES CHANSONNIERS DE MONTMARTRE has an even more interesting history. Verneau appears to be the original printer, hence this is probably the first use of the image, yet it is extremely rare—most authorities do not even acknowledge its existence, only Adhemar lists it as the "third state." Verneau also appears to have sold a number of the lithographs without any text, which is the commonest version, and much later, in 1912, Bruant once again had Verneau print a new edition advertising his appearance at the Comédie Mondain, of which only two specimens are known to have survived. A second set using this image was printed by Ancourt, with the image re-drawn on other lithographic stones, and the text added by another hand. The better known version says only "Aristide Bruant dans son cabaret" and is fairly rare; it may have been used as a stock poster because we know of two specific performances it announces, one at the Alcazar Lyrique, of unknown date, the other at the Théâtre Royal des Galeries Saint-Hubert, which dates from 1899; these are exceedingly rare.

But regardless of the text or lack of text around it, this view of the entertainer remains one of the most powerful visual impressions of the turn of the century.

48. ▶
Henri de
Toulouse-Lautrec
LES CHANSONNIERS
DE MONTMARTRE
1893: Charles Verneau, Paris
38⅞ x 54¼ in./98.7 x 138 cm
Delteil, 348 (var.)
Adhemar, 15 (3rd state)
Wittrock, P9 (var.)
Adriani, 12 (var.)
DFP-II, 827 (var.)
PAI-VII, 330

Of all the posters advertising a publication, LA REINE DE JOIE is surely one of the most delightful. The book, "Queen of Pleasure," deals with a girl of easy virture, and Toulouse-Lautrec chooses to depict her doing what she does best, bestowing her questionable favors on a well-heeled heel. His oily satisfaction, her professional polish, and even the jaded nonchalance of the uninvolved gentlemen at their side combine to make a statement full of wit and irony, as well as profound insight.

But if the uncompromising portrait of what Bella calls "senile lechery" has a sharp edge even on its own merit, without any knowledge of the book or its contents, it was far more mordant in the context of the controversy that swirled around the novel at the time. The lecher, in the book, is a Jewish banker named Baron Rosenfeld; it is hardly surprising that the real Jewish banker Baron Rothschild had more than a faint notion that the offensive character was supposed to represent him, and he made every effort to suppress the publication. It mattered little that it could be shown that Toulouse-Lautrec actually used a friend named Georges Lasserre for the lascivious gentleman, and a man named Luzarche d'Azay for the disinterested party; the controversy went on and, as usual, it only created more publicity for the sensationalist novel.

49.
Henri de
Toulouse-Lautrec
REINE DE JOIE
1892: Edw. Ancourt, Paris
36⅛ x 54 in./91.7 x 137.2 cm
Delteil, 342
Adhemar, 5
Wittrock, P3
Adriani, 5
DFP-II, 823
PAI-VI, 212

LA REVUE BLANCHE was an avant garde artistic and literary periodical founded originally in Belgium by the brothers Natanson in 1889; they moved it to Paris where they were among the first to accept Toulouse-Lautrec's drawings, becoming personal friends in the bargain. When asked to prepare a poster, he chose Misia, the wife of Thadée Natanson, as his model, showing her at a skating rink—which cannot be readily ascertained in this version, but can be seen in a special edition of this image, without any text, where a small remarque at left clearly depicts the full figure of a girl on skates; 50 of those were offered to the public by the magazine at a price of 8 francs, whereas the regular issue was a mere 5 francs.

50.
Henri de
Toulouse-Lautrec
LA REVUE BLANCHE
1895: Edw. Ancourt, Paris
36¼ x 49¾ in./92 x 126.5 cm
Delteil, 355
Adhemar, 115
Wittrock, P16C
Adriani, 130II (var.)
DFP-II, 838
Maitres, 82
PAI-IX, 519

The CHAP BOOK was a curious little publication founded purely as a hobby by two young men from Chicago while studying at Harvard: Herbert Stone, son of the publisher of the *Chicago Daily News*, and Ingalls Kimball. They were just three months short of graduation when they came up with the first issue, in May of 1894: they chose an odd size (4½ x 7½ in.), antique laid buff paper with deckled edges, and an uncommon type face (Caslon). There was literary criticism, art news and reproductions; from the start, the magazine paid close attention to the then still quite new field, posters as art. Moving after graduation back to Chicago, the founders continued the magazine, which became far more influential than its small size and circulation would indicate; evidently it was just the thing for the intellectual circles of the era. Prominent names were commissioned to prepare posters for the *Chap Book*, among them Hazenplug, Bragdon, Leyendecker, Bird and Bradley, and soon the magazine was handling more requests for posters than editorial matters.

In 1896, Stone & Kimball evidently asked their Paris counterpart, *La Plume*, to commission a poster from Toulouse-Lautrec, but it appears they never intended to use it in the United States, so possibly it was meant to advertise the little publication in Europe, although whatever circulation it had there must have been minuscule. Nevertheless, Toulouse-Lautrec went to work, finding his inspiration in the Irish-American Bar in the Rue Royale. The bartender there was a gentleman named Ralph, of Chinese-Indian ancestry, who "with stoical calm served the British jockeys and trainers, and the local coachmen who frequented the place," according to Adriani (p. 196).

The figure at right seems to be Tom, the portly coachman of the Rothschild family, a familiar character who was a favorite of Toulouse-Lautrec's because of his overbearing manners. With only a few lines and minimal application of color, the scene is indelibly sharp and memorable.

51.
Henri de
Toulouse-Lautrec
THE CHAP BOOK
1895: Chaix, Paris
22⅞ x 15¾ in. / 58 x 40 cm
Delteil, 361
Adhemar, 189
Wittrock, P18B
Adriani, 162
DFP-II, 846
PAI-IX, 518

52.
Henri de
Toulouse-Lautrec
L'ARTISAN MODERNE
1896
25 x 35½ in. / 63.5 x 90.1 cm

Delteil, 350
Adhemar, 70
Wittrock, P24
Adriani, 59
PAI-IV, 272

The poster for L'ARTISAN MODERNE, here in a printer's proof state without lettering (which at any rate was added by another artist—see inset), was used to advertise a chain of ten interior decorating stores in Paris. Toulouse-Lautrec chooses to enact a little scene: the workman rudely invading the lady's boudoir, the maid's shock, the lady's placid unconcern at being caught still in her negligee. As an inside joke, the workman's face is that of Henri Nocq, a friend of Toulouse-Lautrec's who worked in the jewelry trade. The name on the tool box, Niederkorn, is that of the graphic artist who handled the lettering.

53.
Henri de
Toulouse-Lautrec
CONFETTI
1893: Bella & de Malherbe,
London & Paris
16⅞ x 22½ in. / 42.8 x 57.1 cm
Delteil, 352
Adhemar, 9
Wittrock, P13
Adriani, 101
DFP-II, 834

One would hardly think that an artist of Toulouse-Lautrec's stature and wealth would normally apply his talents to advertise a product as routine as confetti. As luck would have it, though, Edward Bella, one of the owners of the paper manufacturing plant of J. & E. Bella of London, was also an enthusiastic poster collector who made frequent trips to Paris and counted Toulouse-Lautrec among his acquaintances there. Bella, in fact, organized the first British poster show of any consequence, with more than 250 posters, in the winter of 1894–95. Five of Toulouse-Lautrec's posters were featured in the collection, and CONFETTI, finished earlier that fall, was reproduced as a frontispiece in the catalogue of the exhibition. It is an altogether happy picture, with the girl ostensibly fending off the shower of confetti but secretly basking in the attention lavished on her by the unseen admirers.

TOULOUSE-LAUTREC'S CIRCLE

Unlike Chéret, whose style, revolutionary as it was in its day, was nevertheless easily emulated by his disciples, Toulouse-Lautrec was completely unique, with concepts so sharply individualistic that he did not really have any out-and-out followers in the sense that we normally associate with the word: there was simply no way for anyone to approximate the profundity of his inspiration nor the crystalline clarity of his execution.

There is, however, a group of artists who at least seem to have grasped some of the elements of his technique: bold composition, simple but incisive lines, the use of angles and perspective to direct and focus our attention, the dynamics of unusual framing devices, like the bass viol in JANE AVRIL. Although each uses an entirely different technique, they express themselves in a way that is more like an echo of his style than an attempt to copy it. Some of them, like Bonnard, actually precede him, so there is no question at all of "following"—in fact, the select coterie, even if they did their work after him, did not so much follow in his footsteps as in his concepts.

For want of a better term, we might call it "caricature plus." It is the aim of caricature to make a comment, but it normally does so by distortion and exaggeration; Toulouse-Lautrec and his "friends" certainly do make a comment, but they do it mainly by selectivity and emphasis. It is not meant to insult or attack, either, but rather to sharpen our sensitivities.

Henri G. Ibels

Born in Paris but of Dutch ancestry, Ibels (1867-1936) started out as stage decorator and play producer, then entered the Académie Julian where he associated himself with the Nabi group. He kept up his contacts with the acting profession, designing scenery for the Théâtre Libre and the Théâtre de l'Art and producing posters for their programs. His work was exhibited mostly at La Bodinière, a gallery within the Théâtre de l'Application. In 1893, together with Toulouse-Lautrec, he published an album titled "Café-Concert," with portraits of various music-hall artists. He even stretched his talents to designing costumes for some plays, and later in life wrote theatrical critiques.

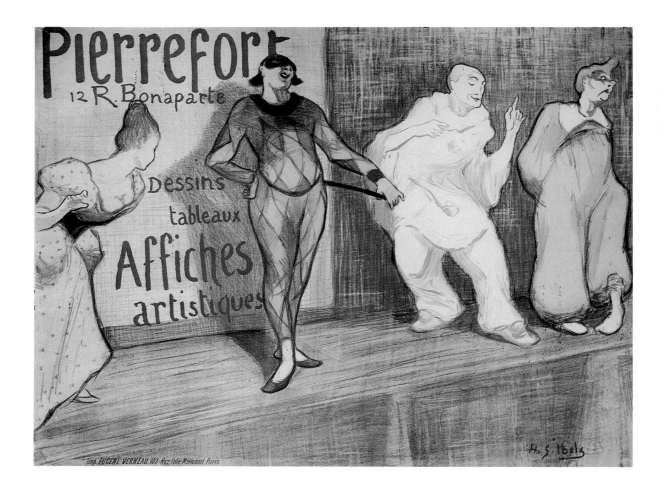

54.
Henri-Gabriel Ibels
PIERREFORT
1897: Eugene Verneau, Paris
31⅝ x 24⅛ in./80.3 x 61.2 cm
DFP-II, 478
Maitres, 102
PAI-VII, 186

Ibels was a man of strong convictions and a staunch supporter of social reform, which led to his involvement with the literary stirrings of the era. He contributed satirical drawings, political caricature and social commentary to various magazines, and illustrated a book by Emile Zola. When one of the minor magazines he had worked for, *Psst*, turned against Dreyfus in the famous scandal, the outraged Ibels started his own magazine, *Le Sifflet*, just to express the pro-Dreyfus sentiment. In his later life, he became a lecturer at the Paris School for Applied Arts.

Ibels' love for the theater can be seen in his design for PIERREFORT, one of the major poster dealers of Paris. While it has no direct connection with the business advertised, the fine visual appeal of the scene makes for an attractive presentation, with the name of the advertiser worked unobtrusively into the backdrop among the clowning performers. The priceless expressions, caught with seemingly effortless grace, bear witness to Ibels' immense talent.

55.
Henri-Gabriel Ibels
EXPOSITION
H.G. IBELS
1894: Eugene Verneau, Paris
16⅜ x 22⅞ in./41.5 x 58.2 cm
DFP-II, 475
Maindron, p. 46
PAI-VIII, 393

56.
Henri-Gabriel Ibels
L'ESCARMOUCHE
1893: Eugene Verneau, Paris
18½ x 25 n./47 x 63.5 cm
DFP-II, 471
Schardt, p. 58
Maitres, 6
Weill, 44
PAI-VII, 185

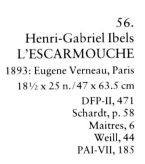

In keeping with his penchant for the theater, Ibels' poster, EXPOSITION H.G. IBELS, for his own exhibition at La Bodinière, shows three scenes from the performing arts. Note the utter delicacy of the colors, and the way they subtly connect the three separate images.

Ibels and Lautrec were the major contributors to a curiously short-lived publication, *L'Escarmouche*, which lasted only three months from November, 1893 to January, 1894. Yet in this brief period, the magazine drew on what could be termed a million-dollar pool of talent; just look at the list of contributors. Ibels himself designed the first cover and this poster. Like Steinlen and others of similar leanings, Ibels had a predilection for the common people, and the scene he chooses here, a typical unpretentious tavern and its frequenters, crops up often in his work.

Pierre Bonnard

Pierre Bonnard (1867-1947) is impossible to categorize: we can speak of his leaning to the Nabis in his paintings, the influence of Toulouse-Lautrec on his graphic work, the trends he was subjected to at the Ecole des Beaux-Arts and the Académie Julian; but there is an ineffable spirit permeating all his work that owes nothing to anybody. It is curious, mystic, introspective, brilliant; Abdy recommended acquiring his posters because their "qualities unfold in the calm of the collector's house."

Like many of the best posterists, Bonnard was a multi-talented artist who painted, designed furniture, tapestry, decorative screens and posters, worked on stage decor and puppet design for two theaters, illustrated books, and contributed to magazines like *L'Escarmouche* and *La Revue Blanche*. And all this from a man who started out by studying law! The art world was enriched when he decided to switch careers, for he became highly influential in several disciplines, especially decorative art and lithography. Widely credited with attracting Toulouse-Lautrec to poster work, he served as a role model to a generation of artists, collected two Carnegie prizes, and was named honorary president of Jeune Peinture Française, an association of budding painters.

Bonnard was only three years younger than Toulouse-Lautrec, and both artistically and socially, their paths were well intertwined. The studio which Bonnard shared with painters Vuillard and Denis and the actor Lugne-Poé was frequently visited by Toulouse-Lautrec. Through Lugne-Poé, Bonnard started designing programs for two theaters where the actor worked, and so did Toulouse-Lautrec. Both men were involved with the Salon des Cent, and both did posters for its exhibitions during the same period (1895-6). They were also both closely associated with the Natansons and their publication, *La Revue Blanche:* they drew illustrations and frontispieces for it, and when it published three humorous supplements in 1896, they each illustrated one (Vallotton did the third). When Toulouse-Lautrec designed his notorious poster for the book "La Reine de Joie," it was Bonnard who worked on the book jacket. Both men were welcome guests at Thadée and Misia Natanson's summer cottage at Valvins just south of Paris.

Bonnard was just 24 when he made his first foray into lithography and poster design, but his initial effort, FRANCE-CHAMPAGNE, was a stunning success. The great poster connoisseur, Maindron, immediately called it "one of the most interesting works to be seen on the walls of Paris." It created a marked contrast to Chéret's colorful fairyland: it was sparse and subtle, making the most of a few strokes of black against a muted yellow and pink background, with ingenious composition and fluid lettering. Some saw in it the first major advance in the art of poster-size prints since the work of Daumier a generation earlier.

Among those enchanted with Bonnard's poster was his friend Toulouse-Lautrec, who insisted that Bonnard take him to his printer, Ancourt, where he immediately started learning the art of drawing on lithographic stones. Thus, while we cannot agree with Octave Mirbeau's somewhat overly categorical assertion that Bonnard's first poster single-handedly "brought about a revival of the art of lithography," it is certainly true that it attracted to it its pre-eminent practitioner. Even Bonnard himself would probably agree to that: once he saw what Toulouse-Lautrec could do with the craft, he largely withdrew from it, creating no more than some ten additional posters in a career much longer than Toulouse-Lautrec's.

Perhaps the most interesting thing about the two friends is the fact that they both learned lithography afresh, and then achieved what proved to be their most spectacular success with it on the first try—all within weeks of each other. And while Toulouse-Lautrec's effort, MOULIN ROUGE (No. 40), eclipsed his friend's work in both immediate acceptance and lasting fame, nevertheless FRANCE-CHAMPAGNE remains, for the connoisseur, a fascinating image, with a quaint charm that is quite unique.

57.
Pierre Bonnard
FRANCE-CHAMPAGNE
1891: Edw. Ancourt, Paris
23⅜ x 31 in./59.4 x 79 cm
Bouvet, 1
DFP-II, 76
Hiatt, p. 119
Maindron, p. 40

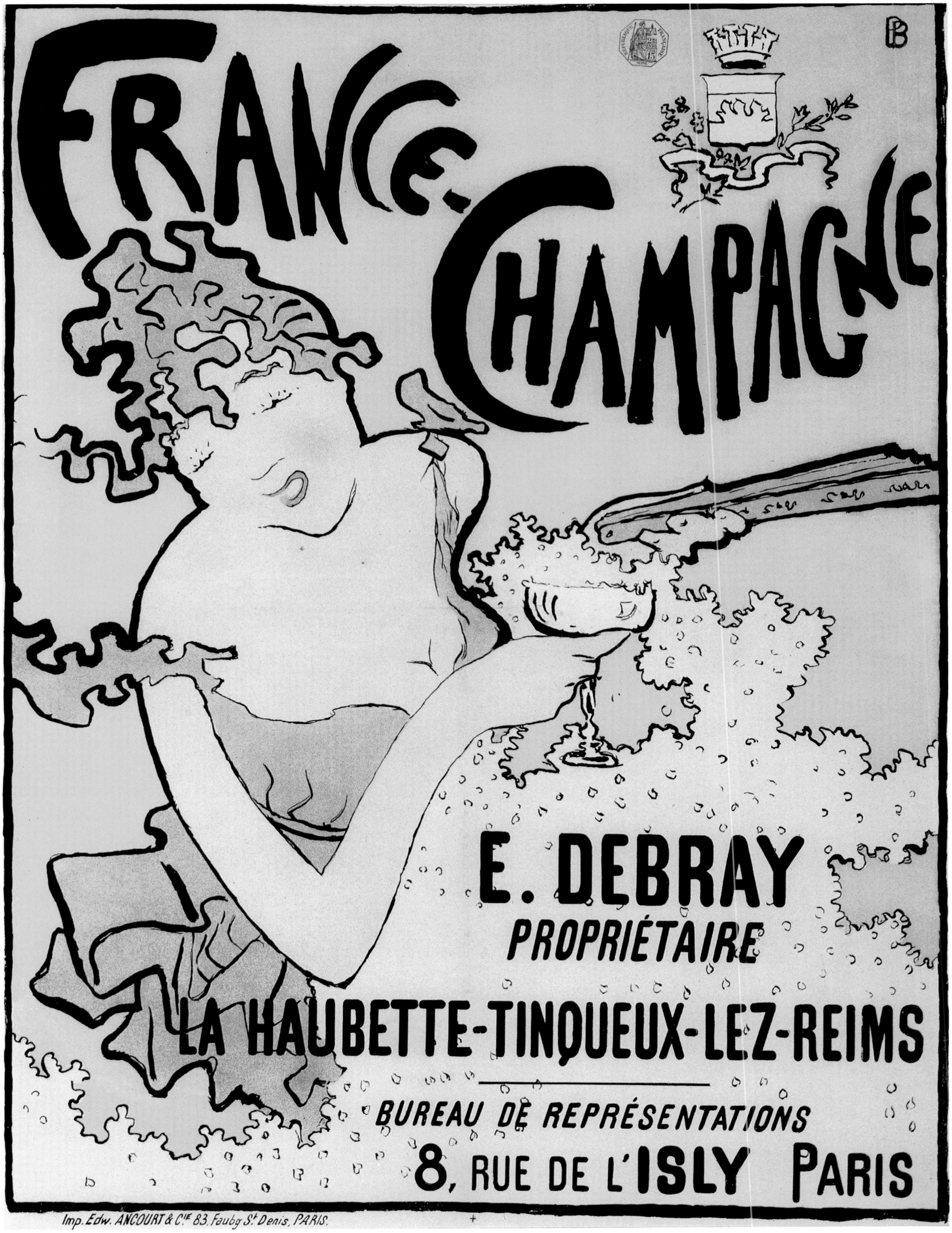

Imp. Edw. ANCOURT & Cie 83, Faubg St Denis, PARIS.

58.
Maurice Biais
FOLIES-BERGÈRE
Ca. 1895: Charle Verneau, Paris
31⅞ x 47 in./81 x 119.4 cm
DFP-II, 74

Maurice Biais

A self-taught amateur, Biais left only sketchy data about himself. Apparently he was entered in the Marine Academy, but his inclination led him to art. He made a name for himself with humorous drawings, and executed a series of paintings for two Paris hospitals. For a time, he attained some notoriety when he married Jane Avril, the cancan dancer immortalized by Toulouse-Lautrec. Belatedly, he became attracted to lithography, and did some posters for his wife as well as other stage personalities.

His FOLIES-BERGERE poster, like all his graphic work, achieves surprising results with the most economical means: simple color shapes against a plain ochre background, and yet the gaiety and vigor of the performance is expressed beautifully. This copy does not include the text "American Singers and Dancers" found on the completed poster.

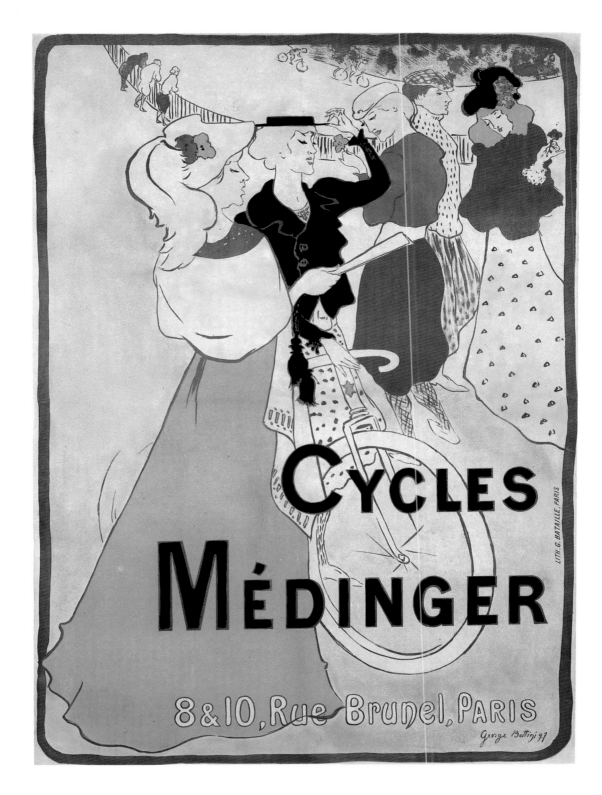

59.
Georges Bottini
CYCLES MEDINGER
1897: G. Bataille, Paris
34⅝ x 48¾ in / 88 x 123.6 cm
DFP-II, 83
Wember, 139
Rennert, 31

Georges Bottini

Equally adept at watercolors, oils, etchings and woodcuts, Bottini (1874–1907) favored landscapes, but the best personal glimpses of the artist can be seen in his scenes from Montmartre, much praised by Toulouse-Lautrec. CYCLES MEDINGER is typical of a fine artist's approach to poster work, more concerned with the delectable young ladies than with the technical excellence of the product. This way, Bottini at least was not risking what had befallen Toulouse-Lautrec only the year before, having his design rejected by the bicycle manufacturer for being incorrect in some mechanical detail. Toulouse-Lautrec solved his problem by having 200 copies of his design printed privately for sale; Bottini simply made sure the issue could not arise. It is regrettable that he never designed another poster we know of, as his treatment shows all the boldness, power and realism that are the hallmark of a fine Lautrec design. But the promise of the poster was never fulfilled; Bottini's career was cut short at the age of 33 by his premature death.

Strangely, the champion cyclist, Paul Médinger, for whom the bike was named, was killed at a young age by a jealous wife who thereafter committed suicide.

60.
P. H. Lobel
SALON DES CENT
1897: Chaix, Paris
18¾ x 25 in./47.7 x 63.5 cm
DFP-II, 542
Schardt, pp. 94–95
PAI-III, 326

P.H. Lobel

Beyond the fact that he was a skilled lithographer and that his work was sold through *La Plume* magazine's Editions d'Art, virtually nothing is known of Lobel's life. His artistic legacy is meager as well, consisting of only a few posters; yet those are enough to show that he deserves inclusion in Toulouse-Lautrec's circle of influence.

The poster for SALON DES CENT, here in a rare version without letters, depicts the 19th century idea of a woman in sports: wearing a woefully inappropriate billowing dress designed to impede free movement in every way, she is nevertheless game enough to try and hit the tennis ball awkwardly as best she can. (See inset for version with text).

61.
P. H. Lobel
PIERREFORT
1897: original design
23 x 30½ in./55 x 77.5 cm
Affichomanie, 5
PAI-IX, 336

The PIERREFORT design shows a self-possessed potential customer examining a sample with a highly critical eye—proof that Lobel could catch a characteristic expression with the best of them. This is the preliminary drawing; the finished poster, only one copy of which is known to have survived, is nearly identical, except that the address was moved to the right. Pierrefort was one of some dozen print dealers in Paris who also dealt in posters, the most prominent of which were Sagot, Arnould and Kleinmann; it was largely thanks to their salesmanship that so many of the fine posters from this seminal era have been preserved for our pleasure.

62.
Hermann Paul
TOURNOI
FRANCO-ITALIEN
1895: Edw. Ancourt, Paris
24⅛ x 31½ in./61.2 x 80 cm
DFP-II, 707
Livre d'Affiche, 122
PAI-VII, 267

63.▶
Hermann Paul
SALON DES CENT
1894: E. Ladam, Paris
15⅜ x 23⅜ in./39 x 59.3 cm
DFP-II, 706
Schardt, 56
PAI-VII, 370

Hermann Paul

Book illustrator, caricaturist and painter, Hermann Paul (1864-1940) took his first steps into lithography in the early 90s under the influence of Toulouse-Lautrec and his fellow students at the Academie Julian, Bonnard and Vallotton. His drawings tended to belittle the bourgeois and exalt the proletariat, such as the series "La Vie de Monsieur Quelconque" of 1895. He contributed copiously to the numerous little periodicals which proliferated in Paris at the turn of the century, generally with political caricature from the standpoint of the radical left. Not surprisingly, he sided with the pro-Dreyfus forces during the protracted affair which divided all of France in 1899, and during World War I he produced fervently patriotic drawings. Paul is credited with reviving the interest in woodcuts—an injustly neglected technique which he employed to publish two collections of war scenes as well as frontispieces for important works of literature.

The self-portrait he gave us for the SALON DES CENT poster has a narcissistic flavor—it looks like he's kissing his own image in a mirror. His only other known poster, TOURNOI FRANCO-ITALIEN, for a French-Italian fencing contest, is faintly reminiscent, in its composition, of Toulouse-Lautrec's MOULIN ROUGE design (No. 40). Both show an artist with a keen sense of visual effect—who else would do delicate pink fencers and flaming red facial hair and get away with it?

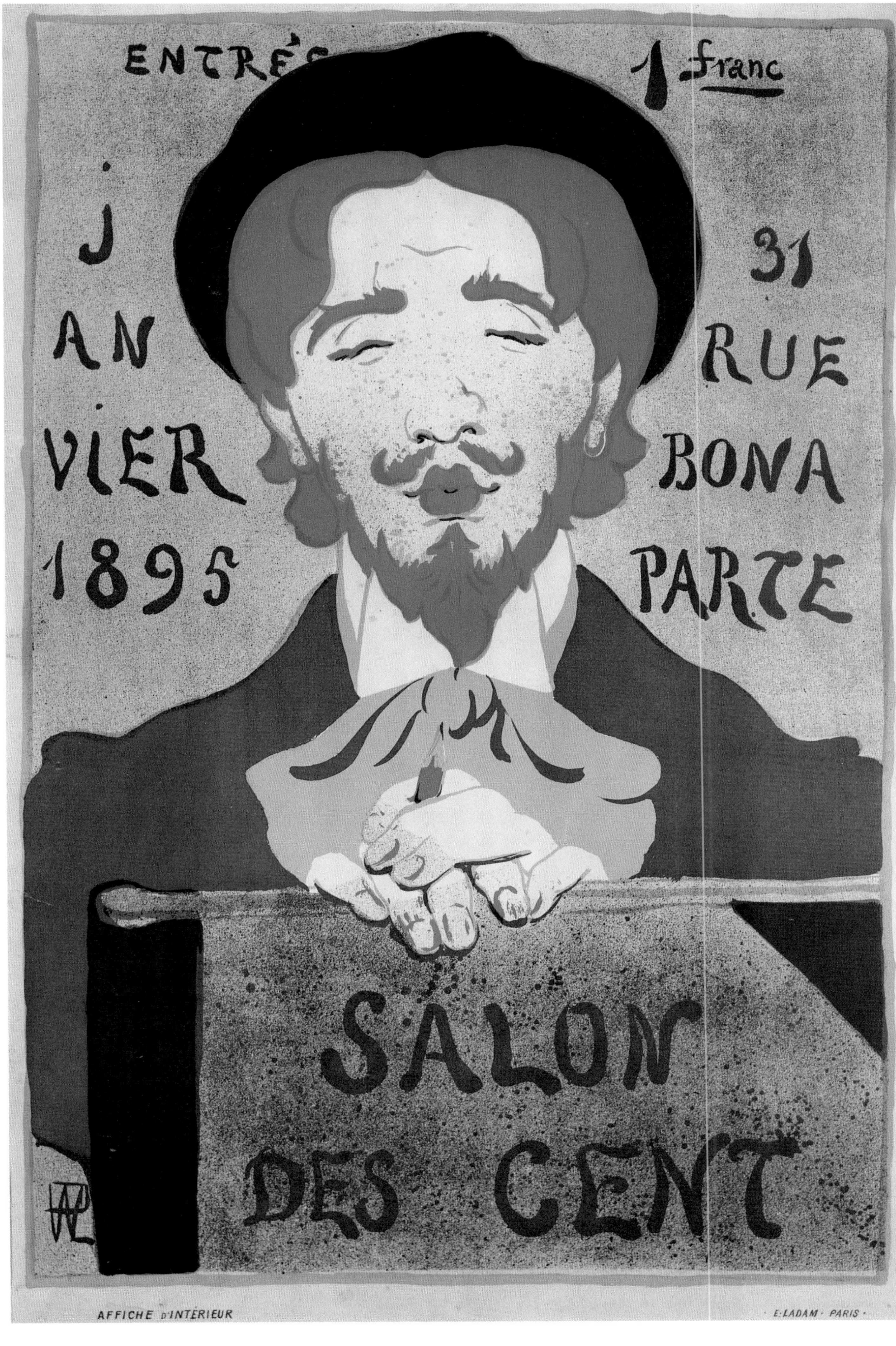

AFFICHE D'INTÉRIEUR

· E. LADAM · PARIS ·

Weiluc

Lucien-Henri Weil, who signed himself "Weiluc" (1873-1947) made his debut in 1896 in *La Caricature*, and went on to other magazines as a humorous illustrator, at first using the name "Luc Weil." He exhibited his work regularly at the Salon des Humoristes, and in the years 1907 through 1909 served as coordinator of the annual event; then, in 1911, he became director of the Société des Dessinateurs Humoristes.

His poster for the magazine FROU-FROU sums up the "Naughty Nineties" with a provocative perfection. The literal meaning of "frou-frou" is "rustle," and you can practically hear those billowing petticoats do just that. Like Toulouse-Lautrec, Weiluc takes full advantage of the sheer white of the paper to create a startling impact. And if the stockinged limbs don't get you to subscribe, those flirty eyes should do the trick. The *Frou-Frou* was founded that year, 1900, and ran until the start of World War I in 1914; afterwards it was revived in the 1920s.

64.
Weiluc
LE FROU-FROU
1900: Lithographie Nouvelle,
Asnières
43½ x 62⅛ in./110.5 x 157.7 cm
DFP-II, 874
PAI-VII, 351

Jacques Villon

Jacques Villon (1875-1963) was the pseudonym of Gaston Duchamp, member of an artistic family: his sister Suzanne and brother Marcel were both painters, and brother Raymond (who used the surname Duchamp-Villon) was a sculptor. After studies at the Ecole des Beaux-Arts in Paris, Jacques started to earn a living with humoristic drawings for journals like *L'Assiette au Beurre, Gil Blas Illustré, Le Chat Noir* and *Le Courrier Français.*

He attained a major stature as a painter: at first influenced by the fauves, he turned to cubism by 1911, together with his brothers, and founded a studio in Puteaux. He belonged to the circle of Apollinaire and Cocteau, and after World War I began to lean to abstract painting. Eventually, he was to gain prominence also in landscapes and in paintings related to his two passions, aviation and horse racing. He was awarded the Carnegie prize in 1950, and in 1957 the International Prize for Painting in Venice.

His lithographic works are concentrated in two relatively brief periods, one around the turn of the century, the other a few years after 1920. Among these, the poster for the Latin Quarter cabaret named LE GRILLON (The Cricket)—note the beer-guzzling cricket in the corner—is not only his best, but one of the most brilliant posters ever conceived. Everything in it works to perfection: the priceless expression and imposing bearing of the main figure, the man at the bar, the lettering which in itself evokes the atmosphere of a smoke-filled bar, the cricket trademark—a masterpiece for all times.

The Grillon was one of the last holdouts in the Latin Quarter, when all the major café-concerts were making a move to Montmartre. The patron with the pretensions of a British dandy was identified as the poet J.M. Levet, a well-known figure in Paris night spots, who eventually settled for the prosaic career of a consulate official in far-off Caracas, Venezuela. The other man in the bar was apparently a singer, Dominique Bonnaud.

The effective way in which he captured the flavor of a place, his incisive analysis of a character, the delicious subtle humor permeating the design—all of them make Villon one of the most worthy followers of Toulouse-Lautrec in the field of poster art.

65.
Jacques Villon
LE GRILLON
1899
Villon, E. 35
DFP-II, 871
Schardt, p. 49
Weill, 49
PAI-IX, 537

Jean Peské

Jean M. Peské (1880-1949), a native of the Russian seaport of Yalta, became a naturalized Frenchman after studies at the Académie Julian and his decision to remain in Paris. Basically a landscape painter in the impressionist style, he attained wide popularity and his works were exhibited in all the major annual salons; his style appears to have been influenced by Pissarro. However, he also dabbled in engraving and lithography; yet no other poster by him has ever come to light.

66.
Jean M. Peské
L'ESTAMPE ET
L'AFFICHE
1898: Gerin, Paris
50¾ x 35½ in./129 x 90.2 cm
DFP-II, 710
Weill, 81
Affichomanie, 52
PAI-IV, 260

Even so, this single rare specimen attests to his mastery of the decorative effect. According to Crauzat, Peské himself worked on the lithographic stone, but the lettering was added by another artist by the name of Riom. The design—two ladies picnicking above a becalmed bay—is executed in tastefully harmonized colors emphasizing the tranquillity of the scene.

The advertised publication, L'ESTAMPE ET L'AFFICHE, edited by André Mellerio, existed for only a brief period, from March 1897 to the end of 1899, but during that time it did much to encourage the appreciation of posters as art for the people.

MUCHA
AND
ART NOUVEAU

Although Mucha did not start art nouveau, nor was he its exclusive practitioner, it was his posters that gave the style a wide exposure, and therefore it is convenient to place him at the the head of this section devoted to art nouveau exponents. Mucha unquestionably did influence a number of posterists to join this new trend, and remained associated with it throughout his stay in Paris.

ALPHONSE M. MUCHA

Alphonse Mucha (1860 – 1939) wrote the book on *art nouveau*, quite literally: his "Documents Décoratifs" became the definitive text on the subject and was used by art schools for a generation. Everything that is best about the style—elaborate ornamentation with themes from nature, fine draftsmanship, the idealized feminine subjects, use of symbolism and allegory—flourished in him to a high degree of stunning mastery. He seems to approach even the most mundane of themes with an almost pious reverence, and he can elevate a girl advertising a common product into an ethereal vision of mystic significance.

Mucha in his Paris studio, about 1901, in front of the GISMONDA poster.

He was born in the small Moravian village of Ivančice in what was then Austria (later, it became part of Czechoslovakia). After studies in Vienna and Munich he came to Paris, where he had the good fortune to be at the right place at the right time: Sarah Bernhardt, the reigning queen of the theater, needed a rush poster when no one else was available due to the Christmas holiday, and had no choice but to use Mucha—but, once she saw his work, he became her favorite designer of not only posters, but costumes, sets and jewelry as well for the next decade. Eventually, his association with her got him to spend some time in the United States, where he made a connection with a rich patron who enabled him to accomplish his life's ambition—a series of historic canvases about the Slavic tribes in Europe.

An excellent lithographer and master colorist, Mucha created about 100 posters and decorative panels and has remained one of the few artists whose entire body of work still excites collectors the world over. A significant number of special exhibits of his posters have been held in the past two decades, and the most prominent admirer and compatriot who has amassed nearly his complete output, tennis star Ivan Lendl, has made his collection available for touring shows—the most recent of which scored a major success in Paris in 1989.

67.
Alphonse Mucha
CHAMPAGNE
RUINART
1896: F. Champenois, Paris
23½ x 69⅜ in./59.6 x 176.4 cm
R-W, 16
DFP-II, 630
Boissons, 30
PAI-I, 217
Coll. Lendl, 26

In CHAMPAGNE RUINART, the lady's face appears in perfect repose, but the hair betrays her, running off in all directions in anticipation of the effervescent effect of the bubbly. In Mucha's hands, female hair achieved a magic life of its own, serving as decoration, framing device or symbol; and if, as here, it could also convey something about the product advertised, so much the better.

Ruinart is the oldest champagne company, tracing its origin to Dom Ruinart of the Abbey of Hautvillers where the process of making effervescent wine was first developed by Dom Perignon (1639 – 1715). At first, the wine was made only for the monks' own consumption, but Dom Ruinart had a nephew, Nicolas, a clothes merchant in nearby Epernay, to whom he gave a few bottles to give to favored customers. The demand was such that Nicolas obtained the secret of the process from his uncle and opened his own wine business in 1729. After more than two centuries of prosperity in the hands of the Ruinart family, the company was acquired by the Möet-Hennessy conglomerate in 1963, but the historic name was retained, and the product is still sold in more than 80 countries.

68.
Alphonse Mucha
MOET & CHANDON/
CHAMPAGNE WHITE
STAR
1899: F. Champenois, Paris
9¾ x 24¾ in. / 24.9 x 63 cm

Möet & Chandon, one of the respected names in the champagne trade, traces its origin to Claude Möet, a wine merchant of Epernay in the early part of the 18th century. Having witnessed the spectacular success achieved by Nicolas Ruinart, who had obtained the original champagne recipe directly from the monks of the Hautvillers Abbey who had invented the process, Möet went his competitor one better and acquired the wine-making facilities of the abbey itself in 1743. By the early 1800s, the Möet family was joined, through marriage, by the Chandons, and the business has prospered ever since under their joint management; in 1962, Möet & Chandon became the first champagne company whose stock was traded on the Paris Stock Exchange. In 1971, a merger with the Hennessy cognac interests was achieved, and Möet-Hennessy became one of the largest corporate entities in the spirits business.

MOET & CHANDON/
GRAND CREMANT
IMPERIAL
1899: F. Champenois, Paris
10¾ x 26⅛ in. / 27.3 x 66.4 cm
R-W, 65
Coll. Lendl, 32
PAI-III, 354

In their relentless pursuit of excellence, MÖET AND CHANDON was among the first business concerns to recognize the genius of Mucha, and used his services extensively to design a series of graphic vignettes used on stationery, invitations, menus and postcards; plus these two posters, one in an indoor setting, one outdoors. The "Impérial" came in three grades, "Dry," Crémant" and "Grand Crémant," and all of them have been advertised by the same design, with the lettering adjusted as needed. Note the Byzantine ornamentation and elaborate jewelry on the dark-haired girl: Mucha was an imaginative jewelry designer with highly original ideas.

69.
Alphonse Mucha
COGNAC BISQUIT
1899: F. Champenois, Paris
13 x 27 in./33 x 68.5 cm
R-W, 61
Coll. Lendl, 31
PAI-V, 242

70.▶
Alphonse Mucha
BENEDICTINE
1898: F. Champenois, Paris
29¾ x 81⅝ in./73 x 207.3 cm
R-W, 58
DFP-II, 648
Coll. Lendl, 30
PAI-IV, 223

COGNAC BISQUIT has an alluring young maiden, standing by a grapevine resplendent in its autumn foliage, coquettishly offering us a drink of the amber potion. This distinctive brandy was put on the market in 1819 at Jarnac, in the grand-champagne area of the Cognac grape producing district. The firm's founders were Alexandre Bisquit and his son-in-law, Adrien Dubouche; it is the latter's coat-of-arms which appears on every bottle of spirits made by Bisquit Dubouche & Company. In the 1960s, the firm expanded by acquiring the chateau and vineyards at Lignères and arranging a marketing agreement with the Ricard interests.

BENEDICTINE shows two girls pressing flowers amid book leaves, to remind us of the herbs that go into making of the liqueur; the bottom part of the poster has a panorama of the Fecamp Abbey where the drink originated. The Bénédictine monastery has been established in this sleepy little fishing village on the coast of the English Channel since medieval times; back around 1510, one of the monks, Dom Bernardo Vincelli, of Italian ancestry, prepared a liqueur using local wine and native herbs found in nearby woods, together with a few imported ingredients including muscat, ginger, clove and cardamom. Called Bénédictine, the potion and its composition remained a secret with the monks for three centuries; finally, in 1863, an enterprising Fecamp merchant obtained the formula and began to make the drink commercially—always carefully maintaining the image of being associated with the monastery.

71.

Alphonse Mucha
GISMONDA
1894: Lemercier, Paris
29⅛ x 85 in./74 x 216 cm
R-W, 3
DFP-II, 624
Maitres, 27
Coll. Lendl, 1
PAI-VI, 152

If ever a single event in the art world could be pinpointed as the start of a new epoch, it would have the be the appearance of GISMONDA on the billboards of Paris on January 1, 1895. Between Chéret's frothy baubles and Toulouse-Lautrec's impudent jibes there appeared a vision of serene beauty: a paean to the most renowned actress of her day presented with all the reverence due a Byzantine princess. Paris was bowled over: an obscure illustrator became an overnight celebrity, and posters were suddenly discussed seriously as an art form in circles which would have before not even deigned to grant them a passing mention.

The spectacular arrival of GISMONDA accomplished more than just launching Mucha's career; it also established art nouveau as a fashionable trend in poster art, and it gave a considerable push to the poster craze which had been gathering momentum ever since Toulouse-Lautrec's blockbuster MOULIN ROUGE of four years before. What had been a trickle became now a deluge: within a year, the first four major books dealing exclusively with posters were written — including Hiatt's and Maindron's pioneering works — and collecting posters became a popular pastime enthusiastically pursued all over the world.

The poster which created such a stir deserves every bit of its fame. Mucha's masterly composition, his unerring eye for decorative detail, flawless draftsmanship, and an exquisitely delicate sensitivity for muted colors combined with his skill in lithography to produce a masterpiece.

72.
Alphonse Mucha
LA SAMARITAINE
1897: F. Champenois, Paris
23⅞ x 69¾ in./60.7 x 177.2 cm
R-W, 24
Coll. Lendl, 6
DFP-II, 637
Maitres, 166

The GISMONDA breakthrough gained Mucha admittance to Sarah Bernhardt's inner circle, an honor equivalent to being granted knighthood by a reigning monarch. For the next ten years, she consulted with him on stage sets and costumes; he designed some personal clothing and jewelry for her; and there were ten additional poster designs, most of them for the plays presented at her theater. LA SAMARITAINE ("A Girl from Samaria") is one such poster, for a biblical drama in which Miss Bernhardt played a peasant woman who offers Jesus refreshment when she finds him thirsting; hence the water jar featured in the design is a prominent prop in the play. The piece was written expressly for the actress by Edmond Rostand, and it opened on April 14, 1897.

73.
Alphonse Mucha
MONACO—
MONTE CARLO
1897: F. Champenois, Paris
29¾ x 42½ in./75.5 x 108 cm
R-W, 31
DFP-II, 639
Coll. Lendl, 40
Schardt, p. 130
PAI-VII, 230

Even for a master of decorative effect, MONACO-MONTE CARLO is a supremely intricate design, with flowery patterns encircling completely the kneeling maiden, and virtually hiding from view the panorama of Monte Carlo and its tranquil beach. The silver ink used on some of the blossoms adds to the bewitching effect. The girl is an example of Mucha's allegory: she represents probably Monaco itself, or possibly the spirit of nature's splendor. At any rate, she's not a real girl, but Beauty; and the flowers, although based on patterns occurring in nature, are not any specific plants but simply Flora. To symbolize and stylize was the creed of art nouveau, and Mucha perhaps stated this premise more clearly and expressed it more effectively than anyone else.

The poster was commissioned by a railroad, Chemins de Fer P.L.M., whose identification is added almost as an afterthought at lower right. Even the most imaginative railroad official must have realized that no feeble words can match what Mucha expressed so breathtakingly with his brush.

A true artist is supposed to be able to find inspiration in just about anything, and Mucha proved this most convincingly in the three designs (one never printed) he made for JOB, a humble cigarette paper. All three offer beautiful women: the unpublished version has an angelic vision soaring above the world, the other two are more earthbound but still far from being just ordinary mortals.

74.
Alphonse Mucha
JOB
1898: F. Champenois, Paris
41⅛ x 60½ in./104.5 x 155.5 cm
R-W, 51
DFP-II, 634
Weill, p. 42
Schardt, pp.140–141
Coll. Lendl, 49
PAI-VII, 237

IMP. F. CHAMPENOIS. 66.Boul.ᵗ Sᵗ Michel.PARIS

All four of the most conspicuous elements in Mucha's poster work are represented here:

1. Woman as idealized Beauty. Nearly all his designs feature lovely females, with perhaps half a dozen exceptions, and they are always shown as embodiments of all that is beautiful and desirable.

2. A circular pattern. A repeated characteristic of Mucha's best work is a bordered ring behind the main subject. Steeped as he was in religious piety, and familiar with mythology and medieval symbolism, Mucha saw the circle representing a halo, the most perfect shape in nature, and perhaps even other mythical symbols of obscure significance––but whatever it was, he used it whenever possible.

3. Undulating tresses. As already noted, Mucha endowed his women with supernatural hair that meanders, flows, frames or surrounds but always, first and foremost, ornaments, adorns and enhances their loveliness. In this poster, it is extraordinary even by his standards.

4. Meticulous ornamentation. Always paying minute attention even to the smallest details, Mucha the decorator makes sure that the background of his posters is as carefully crafted as the main feature. Note how here, for instance, he worked the initials JOB into the seemingly random wallpaper style background pattern, and even into the clasp on the girl's dress.

As poster collecting became popular, more and more homes were being decorated with posters, but there was often some reluctance to bring an obtrusive advertising message into one's house. Printers found it convenient, in many instances, to run off a portion of the poster order without the lettering, to be sold as art for the home; these editions were also often done on special paper or even on cloth, and it proved to be a lucrative supplement to the printers' and art dealers' income.

From there it was but a small step to commissioning posterists to prepare designs that were never meant to serve any purpose but as decorative panels; for the most part, these designs came in sets of two or more, using any convenient theme that lent itself to such treatment: the

75.
Alphonse Mucha
PRECIOUS STONES:
TOPAZ
RUBY
EMERALD
AMETHYST
1902: F. Champenois, Paris
Each: 10⅜ x 24⅝ in. /
  26.4 x 62.5 cm
R-W, 73
Coll. Lendl, 76
PAI-VI, 168

L'AMÉTHYSTE

L'ÉMERAUDE

seasons, the Muses, the Graces, etc. Not surprisingly, the process also worked the other way, and some of the designs, having already proved popular with the public, were later used again, with added letters, as real posters, calendars or advertisements.

Mucha's printer, Champenois, was especially inventive in multiple uses of poster designs, and tirelessly urged the artist to produce decorative sets when he was not actually at work for a specific commercial client. PRECIOUS STONES is one such set, originally published in a handsome portfolio with a special cover (also designed by Mucha—see inset). In each case, Mucha as usual depicts a beautiful woman to personify each gem, and its characteristic color sounds the dominant note in her dress, the decor, and the flowers surrounding her.

THE ARTS was the highest priced graphic work of Mucha's during his tenure with Champenois: 30 francs on paper, and a whopping 75 francs for a deluxe edition printed on silk. It remains one of his finest accomplishments: a quartet of beguiling muses, haloed by crescents of elaborate design.

POETRY sits in a contemplative mood under a laurel branch, looking for inspiration toward the evening star. DANCE cavorts breezily in a flimsy wisp of a garment, her hair gyrating wildly to keep up with her movements. PAINTING is immersed in gazing at a flower, which inspires her to envision whole rainbows of colors radiating from it. MUSIC listens enraptured to the sound of a few songbirds on a branch of a nearby tree.

76.
Alphonse Mucha
THE ARTS: POETRY
               DANCE
               PAINTING
               MUSIC

1898: F. Champenois, Paris

Each: 15¼ x 23½ in./
38.7 x 59.6 cm

R-W, 54
Coll. Lendl, 70
PAI-VI, 155b

77.
Alphonse Mucha
TIMES OF THE DAY:
EVENING REVERIE
NIGHTLY REST
1899: F. Champenois, Paris
Each: 14¼ x 40¼ in. / 36.3 x 102.2 cm
R-W, 62
Coll. Lendl, 71
PAI-V, 240

The set titled TIMES OF THE DAY consists of four panels: Morning Awakening, Daytime Dash, Evening Reverie and Nightly Rest; only the last two are included here. Each part of the day is personified by one of Mucha's unsurpassable beauties; each is placed in a frame of such exquisite workmanship that it creates almost the effect of a stained-glass window. Note that while the borders are identical, the floral patterns are worked out differently for each panel.

As was the case with most sets, there were several editions of these panels in two different sizes, and another with all four panels on a single sheet: that set includes an ornamental legend under each picture, identifying it in fine lettering scripted by Mucha. Finally, there are some sets in circulation where the bottom text panel is left blank, evidently in the hope that some client will have his business copy printed there and use it for publicity.

DECORATIVE
MASTERS

When Mucha startled all Paris with his decoratively drawn posters, it seemed like the whole art nouveau sprang in full bloom from his brush. Actually, this is not so, as the principles of the decorative style had been known for some time and were being used by a few artists; but Mucha stated them with such freshness and clarity that all the others suddenly seemed like his disciples or followers. In reality, the posterists in this section derived their style from different sources, each taking a path of his own. What they all have in common is that they view reality through a prism of esthetics, using whatever beautiful patterns they find in nature to embellish and enhance it, and thereby place it on a higher, idealized plane.

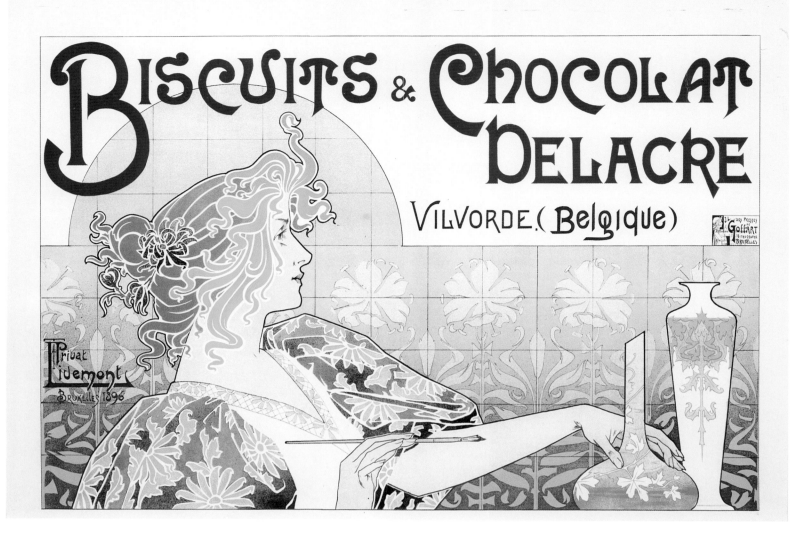

78.
Privat Livemont
BISCUITS &
CHOCOLAT DELACRE
1896: J. L. Goffart, Bruxelles
32⅜ x 22 in. / 82.2 x 56 cm
DFP-II, 1063
Wallonie, 106
PAI-VIII, 414

Privat Livemont

By 1898, *The Poster* magazine was calling Privat Livemont "the uncontested master of Belgian posterists." He had dazzled the poster world with delicately drawn designs which, while conceived somewhat differently from Mucha's, created the same final effect of celebrating feminine pulchritude in the service of commercial enterprise. Livemont (1861 – 1936) could not have been a Mucha disciple for the simple reason that he started out earlier, but he had the same penchant for the idealized female, the same meticulous draftsmanship, and the same mastery of the principles of decorative style.

Livemont came to posters by accident, via interior design. After studying it and embarking on it as a career first in his home town of Schaerbeek in Belgium, and then in Paris, where he worked on decor for the Comédie Française, among others, he returned home and there, on a whim, entered a contest for a poster for the local art appreciation society. To his own surprise, he won: this got him interested in lithography, and before long, he had his own studio in Brussels. Eventually, he abandoned the field to devote himself to painting in oils; but for the few years he stayed with posters, he produced a number of designs of pristine beauty, nearly always exalting lovely young ladies.

One such may be found on the design for BISCUITS & CHOCOLAT DELACRE, painting a vase. Note that the product is not shown; yet such is the appeal of the composition that the company is still using this design on product boxes.

For BOLS liqueurs, Livemont created one of his best compositions, an elegant hostess pouring the after-dinner drinks. One of his idiosyncrasies is the white border around peoples' silhouettes, which gives the subjects an extra glow. The grape leaves on a rich emerald background provide a good contrast. This turned out to be his rarest poster: in fact, there are only three known copies—the other two being in museums in Antwerp and Amsterdam.

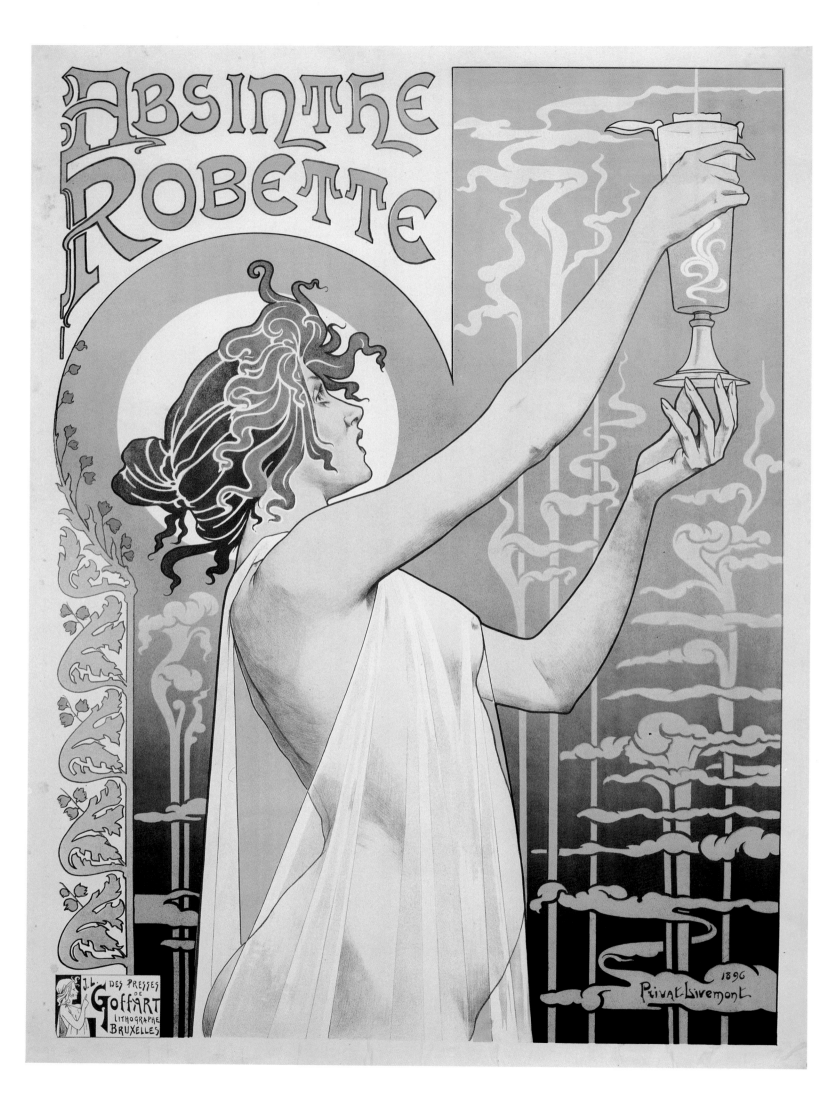

81.
Privat Livemont
BITTER ORIENTAL
1897: J. L. Goffart, Bruxelles
31¾ x 43½ in./80.6 x 110.4 cm
Belle Epoque 1970, 82
Belgische Affiche, p. 197

◄ 80.
Privat Livemont
ABSINTHE ROBETTE
1896: J. L. Goffart, Bruxelles
31¾ x 43¼ in./80.6 x 109.8 cm
DFP-II, 1062
Maitres, 104
Belle Epoque 1970, 75
PAI-VI, 144

More green, shading from chartreuse to olive, can be seen in the ABSINTHE ROBETTE poster: absinthe, after all, was known as The Green Fairy. It was a potent hallucinogen, which Livemont hints at by having the girl hold the drink in an attitude of mystic awe, as well as by the use of a strangely convoluted pattern in the background. A classic of inspired product promotion!

In contrast with the previous images, where the women had short hairdos, BITTER ORIENTAL has a girl with hair meandering about in luxuriant abundance, almost in Mucha's style. Another similarity is the circular motif in the ornamentation—and then again, there is Livemont's characteristic white outline and distinctive lettering. The Oriental bitter was basically gin with a flavoring of various herbs.

82.
Privat Livemont
RAJAH
1899
16 x 29 in./40.6 x 73.5 cm
DFP-II, 1071
Belle Epoque 1970, 87
Hillier, 175
PAI-VIII, 430

RAJAH has the essential art nouveau woman, dressed in bejeweled opulence, holding a cup of tea whose steam rises to spell out the product's name. The hair is long again, but otherwise fairly tame. The Rajah brand name was used for both coffee and tea.

83.
Privat Livemont
VAN HOUTEN'S
CACAO
1897: L. Van Leer, Amsterdam
12⅛ x 30 in./30.8 x 76.2 cm
DFP-II, 1065
Belle Epoque 1970, 85
Belle Epoque 1980, 93
PAI-VII, 204

The magazine *L'Estampe et l'Affiche* grew ecstatic when the VAN HOUTEN poster came out:

"It's a suave young lady, with a wild head of hair, lifting, in a graceful manner, a cup of steaming cocoa, whose escaping vapors frame this delectable painting. A light and silky garment, in yellow, clear and green tints, with here and there some chrysanthemums strewn about as usual, reveals to the spellbound eye the pure lines of a young and graceful body." (1898, p. 16.)

There was nothing wrong with the writer's vision: his assessment is as valid now as it was then. This is the Dutch text version of the poster, which also came out in English and French, and very likely other languages.

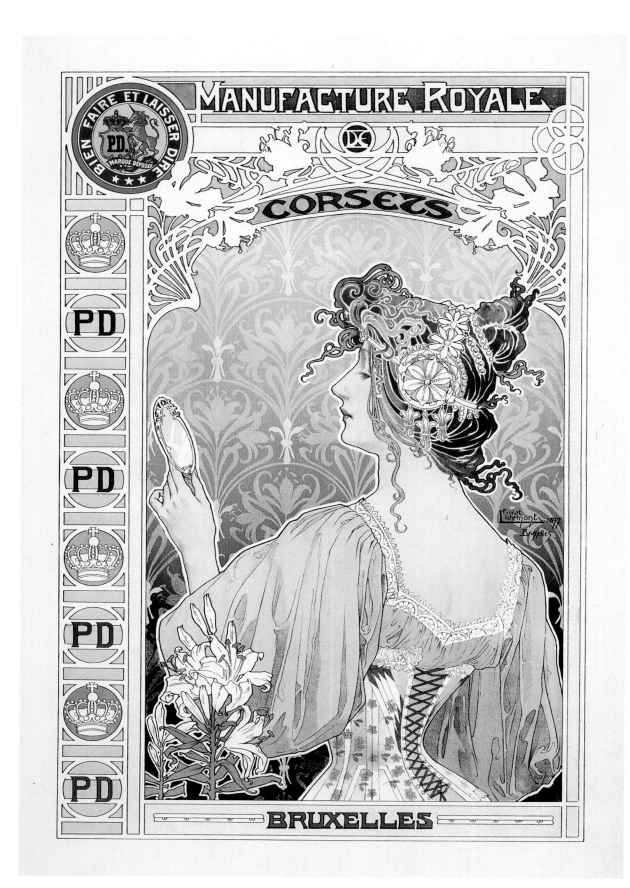

84.
Privat Livemont
MANUFACTURE
ROYALE DE CORSETS
1897
19¾ x 28⅛ in./50.2 x 71.5 cm
Belle Epoque 1970, 83
DFP-II, 1066
PAI-VI, 142

In MANUFACTURE ROYALE DE CORSETS, Livemont is at his best, making the simple act of trying on an undergarment into a scene of serene beauty. In this case, the hair is all piled up on top of the head, held there by a headband of exotic design, but we get the feeling that, once the dressing is completed, the glory of these tresses will come cascading out.

Georges de Feure

The son of a Dutch architect living in Paris, Georges van Sluiters (1868 – 1943) was influenced mainly by the symbolist painters of his day, and his first watercolors were shown at a symbolist exhibition of 1892. As a posterist, he started out leaning strongly to Chéret's graphic techniques, but slowly evolved his own style. He used the pseudonym "van Feuren" at first, later changing it to "de Feure."

Interested in many facets of applied art, De Feure designed wall decor, tapestries, furniture, glass and jewelry, and for a time devoted himself to stage decor, designing some sets for the cabaret Chat Noir; in fact, during his 15-year sojourn in London (1913 – 1928), theatrical design was his principal source of income.

During the 1890s, however, he was one of the most original poster designers in the art nouveau vein, always ready to take an established premise and carry it to his own conclusion. The theme of much of his poster work are somewhat enigmatic women of strong facial features, but unlike most of his colleagues, he does not necessarily flatter them: the mystique he gives them is not so much one of allure as one of character. In some we can perceive almost Oriental fatalism, in others slyness, mystery, or perhaps a touch of sadness, but always a certain detachment. Perhaps because of this unfathomable aura, Abdy called him "the poet of the poster."

85.
Georges de Feure
LES MONTMARTROISES
1894: Edw. Ancourt, Paris
31⅜ x 11½ in./79.7 x 29.2 cm
Maindron, p. 64
DFP-II, 344
PAI-VII, 147

LES MONTMARTROISES is an extremely rare design of de Feure's, from his Chat Noir days, and something of an exception as a woman is not the sole subject. It advertises a book of poems and song by one of the cabaret's frequenters and occasional performers, Jean Goudezki, who is shown in a formal black suit, leaning on an upright piano, giving the patrons a recital of his poetry. De Feure makes no attempt to persuade us that the habitues are enthralled; in fact, they seem to lounge around rather indifferently, which is probably a good indication of how such a recitation might go in reality, but it is refreshing candor on the part of the posterist nonetheless.

86.
Georges De Feure
LA DEPECHE/
HAN D'ISLANDE
1902: J. Minot, Pairs
31½ x 78 in./80 x 198.1 cm
PAI-VI, 97

Another rarity is his poster for the Toulouse daily LA DEPECHE, announcing a serialization of Victor Hugo's first novel, "Han d'Islande" ("Hans of Iceland"). The design features a highly elegant lady, portrayed in a style reminiscent of Japanese prints, against a neutral beige background. Even the oddly angular lettering hints at the Oriental influence. This is one of De Feure's last posters before he started devoting himself to other pursuits, mainly theatrical design, furniture and ceramics, with which he remained for the rest of his life.

87.
Georges De Feure
SALON DES CENT
1894: Bourgerie, Paris
16¼ x 24½ in,/41.2 x 62.2 cm
DFP-II, 343
Maitres, 10
Maindron, p. 63
Hiatt, p. 124
PAI-V, 170

There is an original painting by De Feure titled "La Botaniste" in which this woman, contemplating a flower with intense concentration, faces left, and is surrounded by many more flowers. To create this powerful poster advertising an exhibition at the SALON DES CENT, De Feure simply transferred the woman's image faithfully on the lithographic stone and eliminated some of the foliage; naturally, when printed, the image came out reversed. In addition, other than her flesh tones, all the colors are altered; even the eyes are changed from blue to brown. (See inset for version with text).

89.
Georges De Feure
PIERREFORT
1898: Chaix, Paris
32 x 24⅜ in./81.3 x 62 cm
DFP-II, 354
Weill, 52
PAI-VIII, 351

◄88.
Georges De Feure
LITHOGRAPHIES
ORIGINALES
1896
16⅞ x 23⅛ in./42.7 x 58.7 cm
DFP-II, 355
PAI-VII, 148

To advertise LITHOGRAPHIES ORIGINALES, De Feure created a highly decorative poster in subtle pastel tones. Note, for example, how the yellows are made much more lustrous and vivid by being contrasted with nothing but grays; there being no other colors present, the effect is one of restraint and gentility, a mark of patrician good taste. Obviously, only the cultural elite would appreciate this publication, and the lady with the appraising look is a fair specimen of the clientele he seeks. The proof she is holding has come fresh off the lithographic stone, seen at lower right.

The lady pointing to one of the items available from print and poster dealer PIERREFORT is one of De Feure's enigmatic women: her face is alluring yet inscrutable, with a touch of slyness or private amusement: is she mocking us, taunting us, or simply being ambiguous? To make sure we don't miss her, De Feure bathes everything else in gray obscurity.

The importance of Pierrefort to the poster movement can be judged from the fact that he always used the very best artists to advertise his dealership; see also Ibels' (No. 54) and Lobel's (No. 61) versions.

◀ 90.
Anonymous
CHAMPAGNE LOUIS
ROYER
Ca. 1898
10⅝ x 24⅜ in./27 x 62 cm

Anonymous

The anonymous artist who designed the CHAMPAGNE LOUIS ROYER poster was obviously an obedient disciple of Mucha's; the workmanship on the details of the lady's dress, the minute attention to ornamental framing of the image, even such touches as the hem of the dress overlapping the border, attest to the fact that he (or she) studied Mucha's techniques carefully and diligently. All it lacks is the original flair of the master—but that, alas, cannot be transmitted via an instruction book. Still, this is a fine example of art nouveau in full bloom.

91.
Emmanuel Orazi
LIGUE VINICOLE
DE FRANCE
Ca. 1900: Charles Verneau, Paris
53½ x 38¼ in./136 x 97.2 cm
PAI-II, 199

Emmanuel Orazi

Emmanuel Orazi (1860-1934) was a native of Rome who spent most of his adulthood in Paris as a graphic and decorative artist. To make a living, he supplied illustrations to various magazines, notably *Paris-Noel, Le Figaro Illustré* and *L'Assiette au Beurre*, starting in 1892. Eventually, he landed a steady position with the prestigious art and home decor store, La Maison Moderne, for whom he designed jewelry—as well as one of his best posters. In painting and in poster design he favored somewhat exotic themes with art nouveau overtones.

In LIGUE VINICOLE DE FRANCE, the little cherub dipping his arrow of love in freshly squeezed wine makes for an appealing image promoting the French Wine Guild. Note Orazi's sure hand with colors—one of the prominent characteristics of the posterist.

92.
Emmanuel Orazi
L'HIPPODROME
Ca. 1905: Société d'Impressions
d'Art Industriel, Paris
15⅛ x 22⅝ in./38.4 x 57 cm
DFP-II, 676a

Exotic is surely the word for the costume worn by the rider in the poster for the HIPPO-DROME. We sincerely hope that it sprang purely out of the artist's imagination — we'd hate to see what a horse might do if someone attempted to mount it with such a collection of jangling hardware.

93.
Theodore van Rysselberghe
LA LIBRE ESTHETIQUE
1897: Monnom, Bruxelles
27⅛ x 36⅝ in./69 x 93 cm
DFP-II, 1127
Belle Epoque 1970, 133
PAI-VII, 296

Theodore van Rysselberghe

Theodore van Rysselberghe (1862-1926) studied art both in his home town of Ghent and in Brussels, and traveled extensively in search of inspiration. He became a well regarded painter in the impressionist and neo-impressionist styles, specializing in landscapes, seascapes and portraits; in graphic arts, he was an adherent of William Morris' Arts and Crafts Movement. In 1884, he became a charter member of the art society Les Vingt, which ten years later merged with the larger group, LA LIBRE ESTHETIQUE, for whose 1897 salon he created one of his best posters. He used his own wife as model for the lady seen only from the back; the other woman is the wife of Octave Maus, the founder of the group. Note how the strong warm colors of the ladies' outfits are perfectly balanced with the neutral olive green of the background.

Le Sillon

AFFICHES D'ART O. DE RYCKER & Cⁱᵉ BRUXELLES

◀ 94.
Fernand Toussaint
LE SILLON
1895: O. de Rycker, Bruxelles
33 x 42 in./83.9 x 106.6 cm
DFP-II, 1130
Belle Epoque 1970, 127
Belgische Affiche, 149
Maitres, 80
Weill, 87
PAI-VIII, 533

Fernand Toussaint

Fernand Toussaint (1873-1955), a native of Brussels, advertises in his poster another one of the small art circles, LE SILLON, which also published a magazine of that name. For its size, Belgium had a surprisingly large number of these art-oriented societies all of which strove for better understanding and appreciation of art, thereby keeping the country's cultural standards exceptionally high. "Le sillon" means "furrow" and it is here used with reference to the phrase "cruser son sillon," or plowing one's furrow, meaning making one's own way—the artist's determination to express himself according to his convictions. Toussaint's style tended to be somewhat flamboyant, and he loved to interweave sinuous letters into the design; as can be seen, his sense of color harmonics is impeccable.

95.
Abel Chalon
CHAMPAGNE
DELBECK
Ca. 1905: Camis, Paris
22¼ x 18⅝ in./56.5 x 47.4 cm

A. Chalon

The winsome young lass in the CHAMPAGNE DELBECK poster is the creation of another obscure artist, A. Chalon—said to be the pseudonym of the Paris painter Georges Abel, a student of Rochegrosse. He was a member of the Société des Artistes Français in whose salons he participated from 1928 on. His style, as can be seen, is romantic realism—but the ornamentation, through sparse, is definitely art nouveau.

C.E. Aldrich

That the artist was much influenced by de Feure is self-evident from the pose and bearing of the model in the HOOD'S SARSAPARILLA poster. Here, however, the lady is not the only enigma; it would be interesting to know how a company based in Lowell, Massachusetts, commissioned a little known British painter and lithographer, C.E. Aldrich, working at the time in Paris, to advertise their product.

Sarsaparilla was the world's first really successful mass-produced soft drink—so much so that the word itself, although a copyrighted trademark of the C. I. Hood Company, became a generic term for any root beer for a time. Etymologically, the word derived from Spanish for "bramble vine"—the popular term for smilax, a Central American plant of the lily family from whose roots may be distilled a flavorful elixir alleged to suppress fever. As was the custom in the olden times, various other medicinal claims were made for the many concoctions made from the plant, which was introduced to Europe by the Spanish conquerors in the late 16th century. But it was the Hood Company which made sarsaparilla a household word by putting the flavoring into a pleasant tasting soft drink to serve as both tonic and refresher. Introduced in the late 19th century, it was a big marketing success until it was eclipsed by Dr. Pepper and Coca Cola. Eventually, scientific analysis established that the salutary effects claimed for the smilax extract were largely nonexistent: the root does contain some healthful ingredients, but they are locked in such a complex chemical structure that our stomach juices cannot dissolve it, and therefore it passes through the digestive system largely intact. By that time, Sarsaparilla as a product fell into disfavor, anyway; today, the flavoring is still used by root beer makers, but without any publicity, as a taste additive, and drug manufacturers employ it as a coating to hide unpleasant tastes of certain medicines.

96.
C. E. Aldrich
HOOD'S
SARSAPARILLA
1896
29 x 42⅛ in./73.7 x 106.9 cm
Phillips-V, 2

IN THE LIGHT

of its
Record
of Cures
take

HOOD'S
Sarsaparilla.

97.
Henri Meunier
CONCERTS YSAYE
1895: J. E. Goosens, Bruxelles
35⅜ x 49½ in./89.9 x 125.9 cm

DFP-II, 1077
Belle Epoque 1970, 92
Belgische Affiche, 108
Maitres, 40
PAI-VIII, 449

98.
Henri Meunier
STARLIGHT SAVON
1899: O. de Rycker, Bruxelles
17⅝ x 34¼ in./44.7 x 87.1 cm

DFP-II, 1088
Belle Epoque 1970, 96
Belgische Affiche, 112
Maitres, 196
PAI-III, 132

LITH. GOUWELOOS. BRUXELLES. LONDRES.

99.
Henri Meunier
RAJAH
1897: Gouweloos, Bruxelles
29⅞ x 24 in./75.5 x 61 cm
DFP-II, 1082
Belle Epoque 1970, 93
Maitres, 156
Weill, 95
PAI-VII, 222

Henri Meunier

Henri Meunier (1873-1922) was the scion of a distinguished Belgian art dynasty: his father worked in copper, and an uncle of his was a sculptor. Henri himself dabbled in etchings, lithographic prints, posters and paintings. He had his debut at a salon in Mons with some engravings at the age of 17; later, at 24, he joined the art circle Le Sillon. He supplied illustrations for the daily paper *Le Petit Bleu*.

His very first poster, CONCERTS YSAYE, used with varying text for concerts of the Eugene Ysaye Quartet, established him as one of the best posterists of Belgium: a serene, meditative design which uses four colors to create a harmony, exactly as a musical quartet would.

Two years later, Meunier struck again with RAJAH, in which the coffee-colored background immediately identifies the product; it was hailed by *L'Estampe et L'Affiche* as "a masterpiece" as soon as it made its appearance.

For good measure, there is Meunier's design for STARLIGHT soap, with the artfully synthesized design of a bathing child; again, two or three simple colors are all he needs to get across a definite visual impact.

100.
Jane Atché
LA CELESTINE
Ca. 1898: Lithographie
Nouvelle, Asnières
44½ x 63 in. / 113 x 160 cm

101. ▶
Jane Atché
JOB
1896: Cassan Fils, Toulouse
42½ x 57½ in. / 108 x 146 cm
DFP-II, 24
PAI-VII, 29

Jane Atché

We know just enough about Jane Atché (1880-?) to be intrigued. She was born in Toulouse, worked in lithographic prints — at first in black and white only, later in color — and earned an honorable mention at the Salon of the Société des Artistes Français in 1902. Her scarce posters all disclose that Mucha was obviously her mentor; there exists a possibility that they were also personally acquainted. We know that a Mr. Victor Atché was the director of casinos for Monaco, and that Mucha created a stock poster for the municipality in 1899, at his friend's request; regrettably, his relation to Jane — if indeed there is one — has never been established. Another clue is the fact that Jane's best known poster is for the same cigarettte paper Job for whom Mucha produced three different designs during the same period, and that it was printed by Cassan Fils of Toulouse, for whom Mucha also worked early in his career.

The Mucha connection is clear from the way Atché handles the dress and the cigarette smoke in the JOB poster. Her concept is a bit less lyrical, though: note how the straight line of the black cape virtually slashes the design in half, with a resoluteness we associate more with Toulouse-Lautrec and his school.

The poster for LA CELESTINE liqueur is quite rare. Since the manufacturer claims the drink is based on a recipe from the monastery at Vichy, Atché framed the picture in a border with a medieval architectural motif, and gave the beauty gazing serenely at the bottle an attitude of almost reverential piety.

102. ▶
Armand Rassenfosse
CIGARETTES JOB
1910: Bénard, Liége
37⅛ x 52 in./94.2 x 132.1 cm
Rassenfosse, 46
PAI-VII, 280

Armand Rassenfosse

Armand Rassenfosse (1862-1934) was expected to follow in the footsteps of his father, a prosperous merchant in Liége, pursuing his penchant for drawing and engraving only as a hobby. But on a business trip to Paris, he met Felicien Rops who persuaded him to attend the Academy at Liége; later, the two friends developed together a special varnish that was for a time called "vernis Ropsenfosse." Rassenfosse at first designed small graphic works like ex libris and letterheads, then went on to book illustrations and magazine cover designs. His posters have a directness and simplicity that bring them an immediate attention.

BOCK CHAMPAGNE uses only one color; it's the girl's anticipation of the cork pop that makes the image irresistible.

103.
Armand Rassenfosse
BOCK CHAMPAGNE
1895: Bénard, Liége
14⅜ x 21½ in./36.7 x 54.8 cm
Rassenfosse, 14
DFP-II, 1110
PAI-III, 142

For CIGARETTES JOB, Rassenfosse uses more color, and for some reason, he has chosen a Spanish motif; it was probably easier, in 1910, to imagine a "gypsy" woman smoking a cigarette than having a more genteel girl indulge in such unladylike behavior. According to Weber, women who smoked "belonged to the lower orders or to the criminal classes... By the 1890s one begins to hear of respectable women smoking, but they were either eccentrics or feminists ..." (p. 29).

104.
Ramon Casas
ANIS DEL MONO
1898: Henrich y Ca., Barcelona
41¼ x 85½ in./104.5 x 217.2 cm
Weill, 134
Schardt, p. 46–47
Affichomanie, 157
PAI-VI, 80

Ramon Casas

Ramon Casas (1866-1932) was a native of Barcelona, where he started making a name for himself as a painter, influenced by the impressionists and particularly by Whistler. But then he traveled to London and Paris where he got caught up in the poster craze of the 1890s; returning to his home, he became one of the most prominent graphic artists of Spain. He was art editor of the Catalonian weekly *Pel & Ploma* (*Pen and Pencil*), edited by Maurice Utrillo.

In 1897, Vicente Bosch, liquor distiller of Badalona, announced a contest for a poster to represent his popular product, ANIS DEL MONO (Monkey Anisette). The prizes he offered— 1,000, 500 and 250 pesetas—represented a sizable fortune at the time, and the competition attracted 162 entries, some from foremost artists. Casas submitted four designs, all declared

105.
Ramon Casas
ANIS DEL MONO
1900: Henrich y Ca., Barcelona
42⅛ x 85¼ in./107.3 x 216.5 cm
Schardt, pp. 44–45
PAI-III, 237

excellent by the judges: they gave him the first prize for the blue design, but the company eventually used the others as well. Alexandre de Riquer took second prize, and in third place was a comparative unknown, Alfred Roig i Valenti.

Shown here is the original winning design, and a much rarer alternate design, this particular specimen apparently printed after the 1900 Worlds' Fair in Paris; whether it had a previous printing is uncertain. In either case, they both prove that Casas deserved his prize: the ladies are beautiful Catalonian charmers, and the monkeys are appealing without being cloying. The critic Street, writing in *The Poster,* said: "His drawing is strong and sure, his colouring marvellously clever and daring, though always refined, his composition excellent." (Nov. 1899, p. 122.)

Clementine Hélène Dufau

Clementine Hélène Dufau (1869-1937) studied at the Académie Julian, siding at first with the naturalists, later turning to decorative style and symbolism. She remained, first and foremost, a painter for the rest of her life: her landscapes and nude studies were regularly exhibited at the Salon of the Société des Artistes Français since 1893, and she was a charter member of the Salon d'Automne. She also painted a series of pictures for the French school system, and did a mural for the Sorbonne.

106.
Clēmentine H. Dufau
LA FRONDE
1898: Charle Verneau, Paris
54 x 38½ in. / 137.1 x 97.8 cm
DFP-II, 313
PAI-VIII, 339

Her posters are quite rare, and the one she did for the feminist publication LA FRONDE remains her best. Executed with rare sensitivity and perfectly expressing the women's desire to be led to something better than their present status, it is a poster with a powerful message. The periodical was founded by Marguerite Durand, which in 1897 was a daring move. That year, women in France finally won the right to be called as witnesses in court actions, but they still could not sit on the jury; the only place where they could do so, pointed out an article in *Le Petit Journal,* was the American Wild West state of Colorado, and that of course the paper condemned as a horrible example of unbridled license. Also in 1897, for the first time, married women could keep and manage the money they earned; up to that time, all such earnings legally belonged to the husband. But such steps forward were still rare: when a woman sought to be admitted to the bar that year, she was turned down for the excellent reason that that profession ought to be reserved for men only. Under the circumstances, the new journal was considered dangerously radical, and its distribution was prohibited in schools, factories, and all public places that the legislature could control. Dufau's poster, therefore, remains a poignant reminder of women's never-ending quest for equal rights.

107.
Adolphe Crespin
PAUL HANKAR
ARCHITECTE

1894: Ad. Mertens, Bruxelles

15¾ x 21⅜ in./40 x 54.2 cm

DFP-II, 1019
Belle Epoque 1970, 39
Weille, 88
Maitres, 91
Beaumont, p. 48
PAI-VIII, 317

Adolphe Crespin

Adolphe Crespin (1859-1944) was a native of Anderlecht, a suburb of Brussels. He became a painter and a decorative artist who designed such things as tapestries, ornamental friezes and architectural embellishments, but above all he was an educator, teaching at the Academie Royale, at the Bischoffsheim School, and at the art academy at St. Josse-ten-Node. He traveled extensively in Spain, England and Italy, and stayed for a long time in Paris.

PAUL HANKAR was done during his tenure at the School of Design at Schaerbeek, where he met and befriended the architectural student Paul Hankar. Eventually, he designed the facade of Hankar's own house, as well as those of several other friends. Says Beaumont: "The poster (for) Hankar is in every way perfect. The principal subject, positioned just right, is interpreted in a very modern style. There are many details, but they are chosen with such pleasure and arranged with such taste, such discretion—in a single word, such tact—that far from removing importance…he lends it more value, creating a particular atmosphere, technical if I may say so. The warm and vivid coloring further adds, if that's possible, to the merit of this print…" (p.48).

108.
Fernand Gottlob
PEINTRES
LITHOGRAPHES
1898: Lemercier, Paris
30 x 45¾ in./76.2 x 116.2 cm
DFP-II, 392
Maitres, 219
PAI-II, 165

Fernand L. Gottlob

Fernand L. Gottlob (1873-1935) showed an early talent for drawing, and exhibited his first lithographs at the age of 18. At 25, he was a busy caricaturist contributing to *Le Rire, Le Sourire, L'Assiette au Beurre* and *Gil Blas Illustré*; he also illustrated a few books, designed a series of postcards, and became a fair painter.

While he was an all-around graphic artist, he executed only very few posters. But in the one he prepared for the PEINTRES LITHOGRAPHES exhibition in which he participated, and which was held at the Salle du Figaro in Paris from January 10 to 25, 1899, he came up with a most interesting design, featuring a woman going through a display cradle with prints. The shadows on the front of her dress, and the use of bright yellow in the background creates the effect of backlighting, and gives the scene an intimacy it would otherwise lack.

109.
Henry Thomas
L'ECLAIR
1898: Chaix, Paris
33⅞ x 48¼ in./86 x 122.5 cm
Maitres, 222

Henry Thomas

One can only speculate why, and regret that Gottlob did not devote more of his attention to posters. Interestingly, he won honorable mention (third place) in a competition involving more than 400 entries, for the journal L'EC-LAIR. With some of the best French posterists vying for the prize, and with a distinguished jury composed of the likes of Mucha, Steinlen, Chéret, Grasset and Guillaume, the winner turned out to be a 63-year old American, Henry Thomas (1834-1904). Painter and lithographer, Thomas was the co-owner of the New York printing firm Thomas & Wylie, and when he submitted his design to Paris, it was more of a lark than anything else—yet it has such a freshness and, if we may be permitted an oxymoron, studied ingenuousness, that it well deserved its stunning success.

CARICATURISTS

Under this heading we have grouped poster artists whose primary means of expression is a linear drawing, in which they set the tone by catching grimaces, gestures and attitudes of their subjects. Often, some features are exaggerated in the manner of a true caricature; but even when they aren't, the approach to the design problem is the same. As a rule, these artists also produced humorous drawings for various magazines or books, either as a prelude to their poster careers or as a continuing means of earning a livelihood. Figures and scenes are drawn generally in simple outlines, colors are used sparingly, mostly in flat tones of the basics.

THEOPHILE-ALEXANDRE STEINLEN

Steinlen (1859-1923) was born and educated in Lausanne, Switzerland, but at the age of 22 moved to Paris to pursue a career in arts, and settled in Montmartre. There, he met another Swiss expatriate, Rodolphe Salis, founder and owner of the Chat Noir cabaret and publisher of a magazine with the same name who gave him a chance to get some of his drawings into print. This started a long and prolific career in which Steinlen contributed virtually thousands of drawings to most of the journals which used illustrations and cartoons. His poster career started in 1885, and produced a number of memorable images, making their point with clarity and insight. He was keenly attuned to the social stirrings of the era, and his drawings always reflect a sympathy for the poor and the disadvantaged, and for all causes that aim at advancing simple human values. His warmth as a person can be seen in the way he often used his own family in his poster designs: his wife, daughter, even the family cats get shown again and again, always with tenderness and pride. The vigor of his concepts remains fresh to this day, and he is among the favorite collectible posterists of the belle epoque.

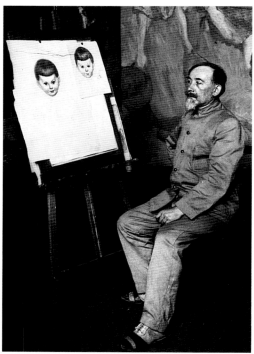

Photo: Roger-Viollet, Paris

One of Steinlen's finest lithographic achievements was a huge, six-sheet poster for AF-FICHES CHARLES VERNEAU. The bustling street scene is alive with an assortment of color-ful Montmartre types, prominent among them the artist's daughter Colette with a hoop, being carefully led by her mother, Emilie. Note how Steinlen shows the working class side by side with the smartly dressed bourgeois, giving them equal dignity—one of his most endearing traits. The design is popularly called LA RUE.

In his posters, Steinlen, as may best be seen here, glorified the working girl. To Chéret, women were ethereal sprites spreading happiness; Grasset and Berthon saw them as angelic visions of innocence; Mucha made them symbols of beauty and allure; de Feure saw in them embodied mystery and evil; in Toulouse-Lautrec's hands, they often personified corruption. But Steinlen saw them as human beings struggling to make the best of it, and gave them his obvious sympathy.

110.
T. -A. Steinlen
AFFICHES CHARLES
VERNEAU
1896: Charles Verneau, Paris
120 x 93 in./304.8 x 236.2 cm
Bargiel & Zagrodzki, 20
Crauzat, 495
DFP-II, 786
Weill, 64
PAI-VI, 198

111.
T. -A. Steinlen
LA TRAITE DES
BLANCHES
1899: Charle Verneau, Paris
47¼ x 62⅜ in. / 120 x 158.4 cm
Bargiel & Zagrodzki, 35
Crauzat, 503
DFP-II, 793
Schardt, pp. 154–155
PAI-VI, 204

TRAITE DES BLANCHES is the image section of a design which originally came with a separate text banner, attached at the top, with three lines of text showing that this novel, "White Slavery," is being published by the daily *Le Journal* in a serialized version. The design shows the callous, flamboyantly dressed pimp and three of his victims, each with a different attitude to her fate: one is protesting it vehemently, another has meekly accepted it, and one is plunged into despair.

Apparently, there was some objection to the display of an ample bosom on the part of the resigned girl; another version was prepared in which the image is contained in a border, and the girl is now wearing a slip; in addition, the red chair is extended to the right, with more text about *Le Journal* on its back. The censored version is more often seen in a smaller size, where the first two lines of the top text identifying the daily is included on the single sheet (see inset).

Nowhere does Steinlen's humanity shine with a greater glow than in LAIT PUR STERILISE, a poster for a milk distributor. His daughter Colette is again the subject; here, she carefully tastes the milk she's giving the family cats to make sure it isn't too hot for them. The cats show up in many of Steinlen's drawings and in several posters, including one he prepared for his own exhibition at La Bodinière; apparently they were very important members of the household. This was the first poster Steinlen worked on for Verneau, who later became his principal printer, and it remains, justly, his most successful one. Its simple domesticity, expressed in warm colors, has never been surpassed; with it, Steinlen assured himself of a place among the front rank of all-time great poster artists. There were several printings, with different text and in different sizes; the Nestlé Company acquired the design and allegedly ordered 10,000 copies with English text. The poster was reproduced in the series "Maîtres de l'Affiche" and uniformly praised by all contemporary poster connoisseurs.

112. ▶
T. -A. Steinlen
LAIT PUR STERILISE
1894: Charles Verneau, Paris
37⅛ x 53⅛ in. / 94.2 x 135 cm
Bargiel & Zagrodzki, 16, A1
Crauzat, 491
DFP-II, 783
Maitres, 95
Schardt, p. 158
Weill, 63
PAI-VII, 309

Lait pur de la Vingeanne
Stérilisé
Quillot frères
Montigny sur Vingeanne
Côte d'Or
Steinlen
Imp. CHARLES VERNEAU, 114 Rue Oberkampf, PARIS. (DÉPOSÉ)

113.
T. -A. Steinlen
LE LOCATAIRE
1913
46⅞ x 63 in./119 x 160 cm
Bargiel & Zagrodzki, 53
PAI-I, 249

This poster, announcing the publication LE LOCATAIRE, a periodical of the Tenants' Federation protesting against greedy landlords and their high rents which forced many a family on the street, marked the beginning of Steinlen's dedication to civic causes. With World War I, which was to create far more misery, already around the corner (it broke out in Europe the following year), Steinlen apparently decided that his income was now secure enough so that he could donate some of his talent to worthy charities. This design is among his most appealing works: the destitute dispossessed family, the older girl already accepting the responsibility of the baby, the heart-tugging touch of the cat, all that is Steinlen at his humanistic best.

114.
Georges Dola
LA CHAUVE-SOURIS
1904: Ch. Wall, Paris
23½ x 32 in./59.7 x 81.2 cm
French Opera, 47

Georges Dola

Georges Dola (1872-1950) was the pseudonym of Edmond Vernier, who was born in a town named Dole in eastern France. Little biographical data is available on him, but he had his own studio in Paris and specialized in theatrical posters, later becoming one of the first to turn his attention to movies. He gained some renown with his paintings, and eventually made some experiments with collage.

LA CHAUVE-SOURIS is for the Paris premiere of the operetta "Die Fledermaus," by Johann Strauss, in its first French adaptation. It is curious that France didn't get to see one of the world's most popular operattas until 30 years after it was first shown in Vienna, especially since it was based on a French work to begin with; but that can be attributed to the stubbornness of the two authors, Meilhac and Halevy, whose piece titled "Le Réveillon" Strauss saw in Paris in 1872. He asked them then and there to help him adapt their comedy to a musical format, but they refused, possibly because they hoped to sell the idea to a French composer, Jacques Offenbach. Strauss went home and had the play reworked by two German librettists, creating "Die Fledermaus" ("The Bat") which first saw light in 1874. It scored an instant success, but it took 30 years, by which time both Strauss and Meilhac were dead, to persuade Halevy to grant his permission to stage the now already classic operetta in a French adaptation. The poster shows a scene from Prince Orloffsky's ball in the second act.

115.
Adrien Barrère
SCALA/
VIENS FOU-FOULE
Ca. 1899: Ch. Wall & Cie., Paris
23¼ x 31 in./59 x 79 cm
PAI-VII, 32

116. ▶
Adrien Barrère
SCALA/MARGUERITE
DEVAL/QUAND IL Y
EN A POUR DEUX
Ca. 1900: Ch. Wall & Cie., Paris
23⅝ x 32¼ in./60 x 82 cm

Adrien Barrère

Adrien Barrère (1877-1931) studied law and medicine before he turned to caricature, but once he did, at the age of 25, he knew he had found his niche. His first success was a series called "Têtes de Turcs" in the magazine *Fantasio* in 1902; he developed his poster style primarily with his work for the Grand Guignol Theater and for the early films of the Pathé Company, where he produced many hilarious drawings for the early comedians like Max Linder, André Deed, Prince, Dranem and others. Before leaving higher learning, he produced six caricature lithographs of professors of the medicine and law faculties at the university: published in 1905, the portfolio went like hotcakes among the students, becoming a bestseller with a sale of 420,000 copies. He was then much sought after, and gained wide fame with his caricatures of French celebrities of the stage, film and public life—the Al Hirschfeld of the belle epoque.

The design for the comedy VIENS FOU-FOULE at the Scala has the unmistakable Barrère light touch: we can tell at a glance that the elderly gent has some designs on the damsel with the hat box. Flat colors and a broad linear treatment simplify everything for our instant comprehension.

Another piece at the same theater stars MARGUERITE DEVAL, who apparently essays the role of a haughty maid; even without knowing anything about the play, we know she'll be a wise-cracking busybody with a few choice putdowns for her bourgeois employers.

Within the poster image:

MANÈGE
PETIT
23, AVENUE DES
CHAMPS
ÉLYSÉES
GRANDS MAGASINS
DE CYCLES
LES PLUS VASTES
DE PARIS
Vente à Prix de Fabrique

LEÇONS
DE
BICYCLETTE
20 F
A FORFAIT

BICYCLETTES PAYABLES EN 10 MOIS

117.
Adrien Barrère
MANEGE PETIT
Ca. 1900: Ch. Wall, Paris
39¼ x 55 in./96.9 x 129.5 cm

MANEGE PETIT was one of the bike riding tracks that were commonplace in the early days of bicycling: you could rent a bike there for a few hours if you didn't own one, or learn how to ride one if you didn't know how. For the most part, girls were the ones who came in to take lessons: if we regard what they had to wear while riding bikes we can see it must have required considerable expertise on their part to be able to master the art. Barrère makes the point with his usual succinct statement.

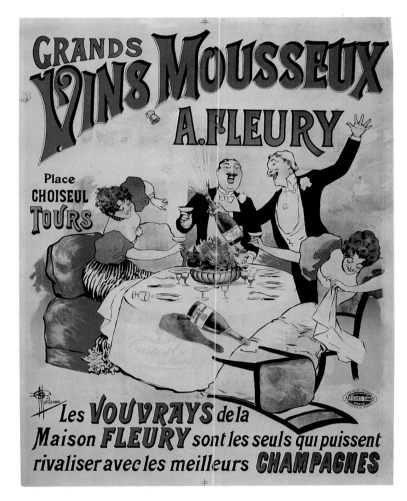

118.
Albert-André Guillaume
LA MAURESQUE
Ca. 1896: Camis, Paris
38⅛ x 51 in./96.9 x 129.5 cm

119.
Albert-André Guillaume
GRANDS VINS
MOUSSEUX/A. FLEURY
Ca. 1895: Camis, Paris
37¼ x 48¾ in./94.6 x 123.9 cm

Albert A. Guillaume

Guillaume (1873-1942) started out as a self-taught caricaturist in his teens, and that remained one of his favorite modes of expression; but later, he also attended some formal classes at the School of Fine Arts (where his father taught architecture), and mastered also painting in oils and watercolors. When he was only 17, he had his first taste of public acclaim for a collection of sketches from the Théâtre des Bonshommes, and thereafter he worked for numerous humor magazines such as *Gil Blas Illustré, Le Gaulois, Le Rire* and *Figaro Illustré*. In poster work, he leaned at first to Chéret's style but then kept adding elements of caricature until he found what worked best for him.

LA MAURESQUE is a good example of Guillaume's approach, a picture of contentment as seen by a typical middle-class consumer: slippers, a cigar, and an after-dinner drink.

In the GRANDS VINS MOUSSEUX poster, the revelry has proceeded a bit further, no doubt egged on by the presence of enticing young seductresses; one senses there'll be some dizzy heads the next morning.

The poster for the pasta makers RIVOIRE & CARRET has a subtly delicious touch of humor all its own: the sweet young thing concerned only with her stomach, the escort anxious to secure her favors, the waiter indicating that he knows the score but is too discreet to mention it; droll all the way.

120.
Albert-André Guillaume
VERMICELLE
MACARONI/RIVOIRE
& CARRET
Ca. 1896: Camis, Paris
38¼ x 51½ in./97.1 x 131 cm
PAI-VIII, 382 (var.)

121.
Guy Arnoux
LES VINS DE
BOURGOGNE
Ca. 1916: Devambez, Paris
30½ x 46 in./77.5 x 117 cm

Guy Arnoux

Guy Arnoux (1890-1951) achieved a measure of success with stencil-colored zinc plate prints and with decorative style paintings on historic themes or serial concepts, such as "Seven Capital Sins" or "Four Elements," and was an accomplished book illustrator as well. However, he was at his best with the light touch: long a prominent member of the Salon des Humoristes, he also helped to organize their annual feasts.

His poster LES VINS DE BOURGOGNE, for a wine merchant, reflects both his preoccupation with historic motifs and his humorous approach to lithography.

Eugène Ogé

Eugène Ogé is known primarily as the house artist of the printer Charles Verneau around the turn of the century. At first, the posters he created were anonymous; later, their lively style began to attract notice, and his name began to appear; he was also asked to produce a series of decorative panels. Some charcoal drawings of his showed up at the Salons of the Société des Artistes Français. The only thing known about his life is that he was a native of Paris, but beyond that, his work is all that remains.

The wide panel for DUBONNET shows the skilled hand of an expert lithographer, and wonderful dashes of irony in the expressions of the assorted imbibers. Ogé was to use the format of horizontal panels with an assortment of characters several more times, sometimes even using a commercial client's poster design to make a political comment.

Jean L. Forain

Jean L. Forain (1852-1931) was co-founder and first president of the Société des Humoristes, but he came there by a circuitous route. His early models were Goya and Daumier, and he tried to reconcile their style with that of the independents, notably Manet and Degas; by 1879, he was participating in exhibitions of the impressionists. His fascination with Parisian street scenes and with current issues, combined with a facility for effective characterization in his drawings, led to his contributing social commentary and political satire to a dozen or more illustrated magazines; in 1889, he even started his own short-lived paper, *Le Fifre,* and during the Dreyfus affair, 1898-99, he and Caran D'Ache started a paper concerned mainly with that abrasive issue, called *Psst!*

One of the many humor magazines Forain contributed to was *Gil Blas*; LA FEMME D'AF-FAIRES announced the upcoming serialization of a novel, "A Business Woman," by one of the busiest writers of potboiler romantic adventures, Dubut de Laforest.

122.
Eugène Ogé
DUBONNET
Ca. 1905: Frossard, Paris
76½ x 26½ in./194.4 x 67.2 cm

123.
Jean-Louis Forain
LA FEMME D'AFFAIRES
1890: Maison Quantin, Paris
23¾ x 33 in./60.4 x 83.8 cm
DFP-II, 360
Maindron, p. 64

124.
Philippe-Ernest Kalas
EXPOSITION
D'AFFICHES
1896: Matot-Braine, Reims
DFP-II, 488
Menegazzi, p. 11
Affichomanie, 21
PAI-VII, 190

Philippe-Ernest Kalas

Kalas (1861-?) has a grand total of two posters to his credit, but that was enough to create an indelible impression on poster lovers everywhere. He did attend the School of Art in Paris, but after a while decided to switch to architecture, and it was as an architect that he settled in Reims. There, he designed a warehouse for the champagne merchant Mumm which was so well received that he was asked to design a mosaic for the facade of the Mumm residence; later, this also led to his designing the Palais de Champagne for the Paris World's Fair of 1900.

Living as he did in Reims, Kalas was lucky to be where an obsessive poster enthusiast, Alexandre Henriot, somehow managed to assemble some 1,700 posters and organized an EXPOSITION D'AFFICHES in November of 1896. It proved to be possibly the most important single exhibition of posters ever held; it gave the decisive impetus to the golden era of posters, started poster collecting in earnest, and gave Kalas a chance to take his place among the great caricature posterists of all time—a chance which he seized most brilliantly. The image was so compelling it was also used as a cover for the catalogue. He designed only one other poster in his lifetime—for the Société des Amis des Arts, of which Henriot was president—and his death went unnoticed by art biographers; but then his delightful poster paster already earned him immortality, anyway.

THE ILLUSTRATORS

The artists grouped in this section employed what perhaps may be best described as a photographic technique: they set up a scene and depicted it with every detail realistically carried out. This is not to say that the same scene could have been, in every instance, simply photographed: the artist does have the advantage of selective vision and imagination. Thus, when Pal shows a soaring fairy showing a bicycle to an admiring throng, he is not claiming it really happens—only showing in faithful detail what it would look like if it could happen. With their realistic renderings, these artists create a feeling of intimacy, in which they ask us to project ourselves into the scene—and this, of course, is expected to make us want to use the advertised product or service.

PAL

Jean de Paléologue (1860-1942) was a member of an imperial dynasty which once ruled the Byzantine countries; by the time he came around, they had long since ceased to be emperors but still lived in aristocratic splendor in Rumania. Pal was born there, got his education and served in the military; thereafter, however, he opted for a career in art, and started working as a magazine illustrator and posterist in London. In 1893, he moved to Paris, at first staying with illustrations; but between 1895 and 1900, he became intensely involved with posters, and during this brief period produced some of the most sensuous designs ever used in advertising up to that time. His loving tributes to feminine pulchritude identify his posters instantly; he could, and did, paint in oils as well, predictably choosing the same ravishing beauties for his subjects. In 1900, Pal made another abrupt move: he went to the United States, and for the remainder of his life worked in applied graphics: at first magazines, later ads and publicity for the auto, film and animation industries. He died in Miami at the age of 82.

For CONSOMME EXPRESS, Pal shows a voluptuous girl juggling bottles of the product. We may not see the connection, but if it made her look like that, we want some of it!

The manufacturer of CLEMENT bikes wanted to publicize their large factory; Pal added a statuesque figure symbolizing the workers, making it clear that hard labor does indeed bear sweet fruit.

125.
Pal
CONSOMME EXPRESS
Ca. 1898: Chardin, Paris
43⅜ x 60⅝ in./110 x 154 cm

126.
Pal
CYCLES CLEMENT
MOTOCYCLES
Ca. 1895: Paul Dupont, Paris
42¼ x 56¼ in./107.4 x 143 cm

127.
Pal
DEESSE
Ca. 1898: Paul Dupont, Paris
43⅛ x 58¾ in./109.5 x 149.1 cm
Rennert, 62
PAI-VII, 384

The bicycle was a major social force in the 1890s. The horse-drawn carriage was slow and clumsy; the train was limited in where it could take you; the automobile was still the toy of a few eccentric tinkerers. But the bicycle gave people individual mobility they had never dreamed of: everyone now could commute to work, take pleasure excursions along country roads, visit distant friends faster and easier than it was ever possible before. Bicycling was an important step in women's emancipation: refusing to accept it as unladylike, they took to it overwhelmingly, freeing themselves from the confines of Victorian restraint. In taking a ride, a young girl could escape the obtrusive presence of her elderly chaperone; and since riding in long skirts and multiple petticoats was virtually impossible, women's clothing was radically altered to allow more freedom of movement. The ease with which women adapted themselves to the bicycle erased the image of them, in both men's eyes and their own, as helpless, inept ninnies: they proved they could do anything on a bike a man could, and it gave them the courage to demand more equality in other things as well.

128.
Pal
FALCON
Ca. 1896: Paul Dupont, Paris
42½ x 58½ in./108 x 148.6 cm
DFP-II, 687
Rennert, 25
Maindron, p. 102

It is not surprising that the exhilarating novelty of unlimited mobility inspired an adulation of the bicycle as a modern-day wonder. Sensing this, advertisers did not sell bikes to the masses as a technical contraption, but as a means to open new horizons of freedom. Many posters from the early days of bicycling romanticize the escapist concept; and none was more effective in conveying the message than Pal. In the brief span of his poster period, he prepared posters for half a dozen brands, and most of the images stimulate visions of effortless flight and power.

DEESSE typifies this approach to selling bikes, with its bold concept of a virtually nude nymph holding aloft the new symbol of personal freedom for an admiring crowd. As befits a goddess, she rules not only over Paris, but the whole world: this is made clear by the variety of ethnic types represented in the recognizable individuals of the audience.

In the FALCON poster, the charming biker is on solid ground, but both she and the symbolic falcon on her outstretched hand still convey the idea of speed and grace. The dark clouds of yesterday are behind her; she is gliding with ease toward a brighter tomorrow.

129.
Pal
RAYON D'OR
Ca. 1895: Paul Dupont, Paris
32½ x 47¾ in./81.8 x 121.1 cm
DFP-II, 688
Weill, 71
PAI-VIII, 484

Pal's sensuous approach really pays off in the soaring vision advertising RAYON D'OR—a humble kerosene lamp called "The Golden Beam." We can certainly observe her beam with delight.

The priceless expression on the clown tells us he's bowled over completely. Probably something about the bottle of CUSENIER PEACH BRANDY startled him—after all, what else could have such an effect on the poor man?

Pal designed a number of posters for various theaters and cabarets in Paris during his sojourn there. Here, the OLYMPIA presents something called "The Fairy of the Dolls," which Pal animates in a bright and lively manner. It is one of his most effective and attractive designs.

130.
Pal
CUSENIER
PEACH-BRANDY
Ca. 1897: Pichot, Paris
36¾ x 50 ¾ in./93.3 x 129 cm
Boissons, 516 (var)
PAI-IX, 401

131.
Pal
OLYMPIA/LA FEE
DES POUPEES
1894: Paul Dupont, Paris
32¼ x 48¼ in./82 x 122.5 cm
PAI-IX, 420

132.
Tamagno
TERMINUS ABSINTHE
BIENFAISANTE
1892: Camis, Paris
38⅛ x 50 in./97.6 x 128 cm
DFP-II, 806
Maindron, p. 108
Conrad, p. 46

133. ▶
Tamagno
LA FRAMBOISETTE
Ca. 1905: Robin, Paris
43⅞ x 61¾ in./111.5 x 156.8 cm

Francisco Tamagno

Tamagno (1851-?) was of Portuguese origin, and started his artistic career as a portrait painter. Moving to Paris some time in the 1880s, he became the house artist of the printer Camis, preparing theatrical playbills at first, later graduating to posters for railroads, bicycle makers and distillers. His style was always highly pictorial, with lively bright colors.

In the poster for TERMINUS ABSINTHE, Tamagno used the likenesses of two famous stage personalities of the day: Constant Coquelin and Sarah Bernhardt, apparently enjoying a toast to a great performance. According to Conrad, the actors were not asked to give permission for the commercial use of their images and Miss Bernhardt, incensed, went to court; as a result, the posters had to be removed from the walls of Paris (p.46).

Oblivious to the sign "3-minute Stop," the pretty traveler is so happy savoring her FRAM-BOISETTE liqueur that the trainmen are getting frantic in their efforts to get her back aboard.

LA
FRAMBOISETTE
BUFFET DE GAR
FRAMBOISETTE
DESGRANGE
DIJON
3 Minutes
d'arret
La Framboisette
GARANTIE PUR JUS DE FRUITS
DESGRANGE
Seul Fabricant
DIJON
LA FRAMBOISETTE
INDICATEUR DES CHEMINS DE FER
FRAMBOISETTE
Gallice Lith.
TAMAGNO
AU VIN BLANC · AU VERMOUTH
AU CHAMPAGNE · A L'EAU DE SELTZ
LA LITHOGRAPHIE PARISIENNE, ROBIN Dr. 27 Rue Corbeau, PARIS.

134.
Henri Gray
CURACAO SUPREME
1898: Courmont Frères, Paris
39⅛ x 55 in./99.4 x 139.7 cm
PAI-IX, 286

135. ▶
Henri Gray
AFFICHES-PICHOT
Ca. 1900: Pichot, Paris
54 x 85 in./137.2 x 216 cm

Henri Gray

Gray is the pseudonym of Henri Boulanger (1858-1924), who started out as an illustrator leaning to caricature for various journals in Paris in the late 1870s, signing himself at first as "Grivois." In 1882, he joined the staff of *Paris s'Amuse*, then switched to *Chronique Parisienne* for whom he designed monthly covers, and in 1888 moved on to *Paris-Noël*. Versatile and multi-talented, he illustrated the catalogue for the 1886 exhibition of Arts Incohérents, designed costumes for the Concert Européen and for the Folies-Bergère, and executed many minor graphic works like menus and invitations. During the height of the poster craze, he joined the band wagon, adopting the name "Gray" and producing a sizable quantity of posters, always with a flair that often touches flamboyance.

The pert young miss is dressed quite demurely, but the taste of CURACAO SUPREME put her in such good cheer she decided to favor us with a display of some fluffy unmentionables.

As to the sprite personifying the printing firm AFFICHES PICHOT, being an allegorical being she can throw caution to the winds and give us even more of her buxom charms.

AFFICHES-PICHOT

PICHOT

IMPRIMEUR, 54, Rue de Clichy, PARIS

Jules-Alexandre Grün

A versatile decorative artist, Grün (1868-1934) started as a painter of still life and portraits, but in the 1890s began to do illustrations for several Paris magazines. Living in the bohemian quarter, he frequented the cafes where artists often went, and got interested in designing interior decor for them; happy with the results, several of them ordered posters for their establishments and for the revues they presented. And that's where he found his true calling: his posters virtually breathe the atmosphere of the Naughty Nineties, full of insouciant flirts, lascivious gentlemen on the make, and unrestrained fun.

The poster for BAL TABARIN is typical of Grün's approach — we can see instantly that, if the three oddly assorted revelers have anything to say about it, there'll be a hot time in the old town tonight. Interestingly, it seems that some bigots objected to the dark-skinned gentleman being allowed in on the fun; there is a second version of the design, where the third man is of the approved skin tone. But Grün had the last word: that man is gazing lecherously right down her dress. Take that, you fool censors!

136.
Jules-Alexandre Grün
BAL TABARIN
1904: Chaix, Paris
37⅞ x 44¾ in./88.6 x 123.8 cm
Spectacle, 1334
PAI-IX, 301

137.
Anonymous
LA MEUSE
Ca. 1900: Lemercier, Paris
41¾ x 57¼ in./106 x 145.4 cm

138.
Anonymous
LA MEUSE
Ca. 1900: Lemercier, Paris
41⅞ x 57¼ in./106.4 x 145.4 in.
Boissons, 170

Anonymous

These two posters, both anonymous, advertise LA MEUSE, the beer of the Meuse River region which supplies most of the French domestic production of malted beverages. When the war of 1870 ceded Alsace and Lorraine to Germany, many Frenchmen began to boycott German products. A brewery near Strasbourg, anxious to retain its French market, accordingly opened a new branch in the French territory, at Bar-le-Duc on the Meuse River, in 1888. Its German brewmaster, Adolph Kreiss, came up with such a superior product that already two years later, he combined the fledgling operation with several other small producers in the region, under the name Société des Brasseries de la Meuse. It prospered and continued to absorb other independents; today it is part of a beer cartel Société Européenne de Brasserie.

The Meuse beer producers often used prominent posterist to advertise, including Mucha. These two samples are by an unknown artist but both were printed by the same printer, and were probably done by the same hand: note, for example, the similar treatment of the glass mugs. Although they are, lithographically, separate posters. they also work well as a single billboard.

Anonymous

An anonymous poster printed for CHIANTI RUFFINO by Italy's best lithographer, Ricordi of Milan, could well be imagined, without the text, as a mural or frieze from the classic period in Italian art. The ever-present cherubs are however relieved of their customary role of hovering around the edges of mythological scenes, and are given a rather arduous task of carrying a length of vine laden with ripe grapes.

139.
Anonymous
CHIANTI RUFFINO
Ca. 1898: C. Ricordi, Milano
55 x 38¾ in. / 139.7 x 98.5 cm

Mathilde A. Herouard

Little is known of Ms. Herouard's life other than that she was born in 1880 in the small town of Le Puy, and worked for most of her life in oils and pastels; her paintings were exhibited in the Salon of the Société des Artistes Français and in the Salon d'Hiver.

The VOUVRAY MONOPOLE poster shows the artist's painterly background, but she is also aware of the needs of a poster and has produced an eye-catching composition.

140.
Mathilde Herouard
VOUVRAY
MONOPOLE
Ca. 1910: Camis, Paris
48 x 31 in./122 x 78.8 cm

141. ▶
Charles Senard
LA GOUTTE D'OR
1895: Fournier, Lyon
39 x 77⅛ in./99.8 x 197.1 cm
DFP-II, 771

Charles Senard

Senard (1876-1934) was an illustrator by trade, but he also painted: his specialty was still life and flower arrangements done in the style of 18th century painters. His only known poster is this design for yet another stomach bitters, LA GOUTTE D'OR ("The Golden Drop"), with a jolly gentleman with a preposterous mustache. To give a more prominent play to the golden liquor, Senard makes the black of the toper's dress merge with the background, creating an arresting composition. If the man's expression is any indication, the drink must be just the thing for what ails you.

Firmin Bouisset

Etienne-Maurice-Firmin Bouisset (1859-1925) studied at the Ecole des Beaux-Arts in Paris and went into portraiture, specializing in children; he even designed murals for children's rooms. He also became proficient in graphic arts as book illustrator, lithographer and designer of calendars.

His design for CHOCOLAT MENIER became one of the most appealing images ever associated with a company. It went through many printings in several languages, and remained the company's symbol for decades. It deserves it—it's an eloquent masterpiece of poster design.

The Lefèvre-Utile biscuit manufacturer was always eager to avail itself of the services of the best posterists. For them, Bouisset has a boy munching on a LU biscuit—and, since the company always tried to project an upper-class image, he put him in the uniform of a prestigious private school, with a smock and a medal for scholarship. The LU-LU boy became a trademark used on product boxes, and it can be seen to this day painted on the entire gable wall of a 6-story building on rue D'Auteuil in Paris.

144.
Robys
KINA-LILLET
Ca. 1899: Imprimeries Réunies
de Levallois
39 x 55 in./99.8 x 140.8 cm

Robys

Robys is a complete enigma; all we know is that his spelling was wobbly—note he spells the product's name with only one L in the bottom line. But he certainly could produce a design with a strong impact, and his draftsmanship is admirable.

Paul and Raymond Lillet lived in the village of Podensac, in the wine-growing region of Gironde, not too many miles from Bordeaux—just where the Bordeaux grapes leave off and the Sauternes begin. One day in 1872, they took some of their locally produced white wine, added a little quinine and about 15% fruit liquor, and began marketing it under the name KINA LILLET ("Kina" being a contraction of the usual "Quinquina"). The enterprise remained a family business until 1985, when a group of local investors acquired an interest in it in order to improve the product's marketing strategy.

145.
Anonymous
ST. RAPHAEL
QUINQUINA
Ca. 1896: Lemercier, Paris
55⅛ x 82¾ in./140 x 210.2 cm

Anonymous

Another bitters based on quinine was developed by a country doctor with a practice in Lyon. Tired from overwork one day in 1897, and experiencing some trouble with his eyes, he mixed himself a drink of wine with a little quinine in it to revive his spirits. It not only cheered him up, but to his surprise his eye trouble cleared up, and after several days disappeared altogether. He recalled from the bible that Archangel Raphael restored someone's sight miraculously, and so he put his concoction on the market with the name ST. RAPHAEL QUINQUINA. The unknown artist shows two perky young ladies eagerly accepting a drink and some biscuits of the same brand name, which must have been at some time added to the St. Raphael line, from a high-class servant.

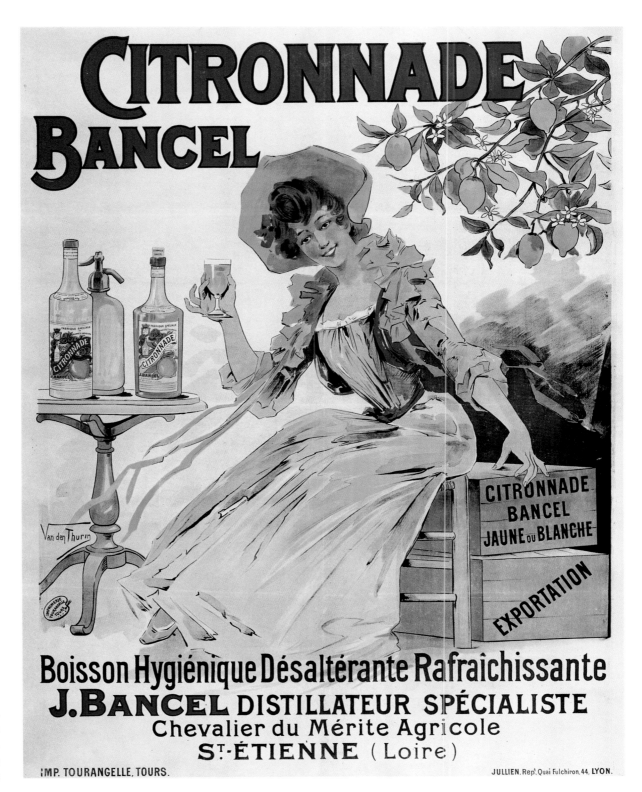

Claire Masson

Masson was the pseudonym of Claire Mallon (1887-?) whose primary interest was engraving in copper; but she also painted, and her work found its way to the prestigious Salon in 1920, when she became a member of the Société des Artistes Français. Her poster is a rarity—if there were more of them, none have surfaced among collectors. It is certainly the rarest of the many posters for DUBONNET; here, we have a very proper young maiden with a strikingly lovely face having a good time in her garden. She is dressed for the summer the way a Victorian lady considered proper; making quite sure that not an inch of her body should be exposed to the pernicious rays of the sun.

Van Den Thurm

The artist left no data beyond his name, but he was a competent posterist: the design for CITRONNADE BANCEL is well composed and has a cheerful, sunny touch to it.

149.
M. Stéphane
AFFICHES BRONDERT
Ca. 1898: Affiches Brondert,
Paris
61¼ x 45¼ in./155.5 x 115 cm

◀148.
M. Auzolle
CHAMPAGNE MASSE
PERE & FILS
1920: Maus, Delhalle & Urban,
Paris
30⅞ x 47½ in./78.3 x 120.6 cm
Boissons, 57

M. Auzolle

Although no details of his life have ever come to light, Auzolle did leave us about two dozen posters, all showing the hand of a careful and imaginative craftsman. It was he who designed the poster for a historic milestone, the first public showing of Lumière Brothers' cinematograph in 1895.

In the poster for MASSE PERE & FILS, Auzolle creates a good effect from the light thrown by the hand-carried lantern. The champagne producer has been in business since 1853, when the firm was started by Charles Masse at Rilly-la-Montagne. It stayed in the family's hands until 1976, by which time it produced about half a million bottles annually. It was then absorbed by its larger neighbor, Lanson, and together they became part of the BSN conglomerate in 1984.

M. Stéphane

In the poster for printer-lithographer BRONDERT, the all-but-unknown artist has two fair maidens, one inspecting a poster, the other one giving it a critical appraisal. Their clothes have something faintly Russian about it, which makes one wonder if Stéphane might not have been one of the Russian emigres in Paris.

Franc Malzac

In 1904, a car was a luxury owned only by a few rich people, which is why having a motorist ask for the product, Kina BRIS, gave it automatic snob appeal. We know next to nothing about Malzac, but obviously he was a capable poster designer; perhaps the fact that he was based in Bordeaux prevented him from attaining a greater measure of fame.

150.
Franc Malzac
VITE! UN BRIS
1904: Charles Verneau, Paris
53⅝ x 39 in./136.2 x 99 cm
PAI-VII, 409

Leopoldo Metlicovitz

Metlicovitz (1868 – 1944) was one of the most active Italian posterists, born in Trieste of Serbian ancestry. He appears to have been largely self-taught as a painter, and in 1891 he came to Milan to join the Ricordi printing plant as a lithographic trainee. A quick study, he gained the position of technical director within a year, and soon was designing posters at a prodigious rate. He evolved his own style, playing with light and shadow, and helping to develop what eventually became known as "bourgeois realism," a Ricordi trademark: fashionable elegance to which the average person could aspire.

In BITTER PASTORE, Metlicovitz shows how ice can be broken during a dalliance by means of a toast with the crimson aperitif.

151.▶
Leopoldo Metlicovitz
BITTER PASTORE/
MILANO
Ca. 1903: Ricordi, Milano
56¾ x 81 in./144 x 205.8 cm
PAI-IV, 83

◀ 152.
Jack Abeille
PETIT-BEURRE GAMIN
1901: G. Gerin Fils, Dijon
38⅝ x 55 in./98 x 139.7 cm
DFP-II,1

153. ▶
Francois Flameng
PARIS EXPOSITION
1900/LE GUIDE
1899
Vieillemard Fils, Paris
32⅞ x 52⅝ in./83.5 x 133.8 cm
DFP-II, 357

Jack Abeille

Abeille (1873 – ?) started out as an illustrator, working on a series of books issued under the title "Modern Bibliothèque" by the publisher Fayard. He also submitted some pen drawings and watercolors to the Salon des Humoristes, and worked from time to time for various humor magazines. His posters are rare.

For the PETIT-BEURRE GAMIN label of the Pernot biscuit company, Abeille here publicizes the brand by having a gamin, or street urchin, beat out the news on a product box serving as a drum. This gamin doesn't look much like a child of the streets, but then again it wouldn't do to have a good product advertised by a real ruffian.

Francois Flameng

Flameng (1856 – 1925) studied graphic arts, exhibiting his first engravings at the age of 18 at the Salon. He then turned to paintings, favoring historic scene, and also delved into portraiture. That earned him some commissions from rich patrons, and he traveled to England and America to execute lucrative orders; his influential patrons obtained for him the privilege of decorating the upper vestibule of the Sorbonne. In his thirties, he returned to graphics, illustrating the works of Francois Coppée and Victor Hugo and working for some gazettes.

In the poster for a guidebook to the World's Fair of 1900, Flameng draws an allegorical figure with an open book to which she apparently wants to bestow a laurel wreath. It is unclear whether she is meant to represent Paris, or the "100 million" visitors claimed by the publishers.

HACHETTE & Cie
AUX 100 MILLIONS DE VISITEURS !
ACHETEZ
PARIS EXPOSITION
450 PAGES 1fr 50
1900
LE GUIDE
LE PLVS POPVLAIRE
LE PLVS PRATIQVE
AUX MERVEILLES
DE PARIS & DE L'EXPOSITION
· HACHETTE & Cie ·
FRANÇOIS FLAMENG · P · IT
IMP VIEILLEMARD FILS & Cie 16, RUE DE LA GLACIÈRE, PARIS.

154.
H. Tanconville
EVIAN
Ca. 1897: Courmont Frères,
Paris
30⅜ x 41¾ in./77.2 x 106 cm

155. ▶
Hugo d'Alesi:
P.L.M./
POUGUES-LES-EAUX
Ca. 1898
28¾ x 41¾ in./73 x 106 cm

Frederic Hugo d'Alesi

Alesi (1849 – 1906) was the son of a French officer who served as an instructor to the Turkish army; he was born in Rumania and lived at first in Smyrna, where he was educated as an engineer. He didn't reach Paris until his 27th year, but once there, he became interested in art: at first as a painter who favored landscapes, and from 1882 as a posterist. His first posters were for theaters and cabarets, but in the early 1890s he began to work for several railroads, which permitted him to indulge his landscape painting style, in more than one hundred travel posters.

This poster for the Paris-Lyon-Méditerranée Railroad is fairly typical of his approach, featuring two landscapes for the price of one: a quiet arboreal dell and a sun-bathed panorama.

H. Tanconville

Tanconville is the pseudonym of Henry Ganier (1846–1936), who worked for the same railroad at the same time. His style is also similar, a meticulous postcard-pretty rendering of the EVIAN spa on the shore of Lac Leman.

P.L.M.

POUGUES-LES-EAUX

F. Hugo d'Alési

VUE GÉNÉRALE DE POUGUES.

BILLETS D'ALLER & RETOUR COLLECTIFS
DE VILLES D'EAUX
délivrés du 15 Mai au 15 Septembre
POUR
POUGUES-LES-EAUX
par toutes les gares du réseau P.L.M. situées à 150 kilomètres
au moins de POUGUES-LES-EAUX

BILLETS CIRCULAIRES A PRIX RÉDUITS

MM. les Voyageurs pourront se procurer tous les renseignements utiles sur les diverses combinaisons de voyages et les prix les plus économiques :

1° En s'adressant à toutes les gares et aux bureaux de ville de la Compagnie P.-L.-M., ainsi qu'aux Agences de Voyages indiquées ci-après :

A Paris : COOK & FILS, Place de l'Opéra, 1. — VOYAGES ÉCONOMIQUES, Rue Auber, 10 et Rue du Faubourg-Montmartre, 17. — WAGONS-LITS, Place de l'Opéra, 3, et Grand-Hôtel, Boulevard des Capucines. — H. GAZE & FILS, Rue Scribe, 2. — LUBIN, Boulevard Haussmann, 36. — SOCIÉTÉ FRANÇAISE DES VOYAGES DUCHEMIN, Rue de Grammont, 20. — DESROCHES, Rue du Faubourg Montmartre, 21.

Bureau Général des Billets de Chemins de Fer de l'Hôtel Terminus de la gare de Paris St-Lazare. (Général Ticket Office).

2° En consultant, soit le Livret-Guide P.-L.-M., (horaires et tarifs de voyageurs), soit l'Indicateur des Chemins de Fer, qui sont vendus au prix de 0 fr. 40 dans les principales gares du réseau.

156.
Georges Rochegrosse
LOUISE
1900: Delauchy, Paris
30⅜ x 41¾ in./77.2 x 106 cm
Maitres, 230
DFP-II, 751
French Opera, 22

Georges Rochegrosse

Rochegrosse (1859 – 1938) gained some notoriety for historic paintings in the realistic style, which in the early 1880s was something of a novelty. For the biggest of them, "The Death of Babylon," he earned the Legion of Honor medal in 1891; it made him the darling of official art circles, and he also won the gold medal at a Munich exhibition. He now started illustrating books for the literary giants of his time: Théophile Gautier, Gustave Flaubert, Victor Hugo; and he joined the staff of the magazine *La Vie Parisienne*.

In the poster for LOUISE, a sentimental romance in musical form, Rochegrosse gives us a couple on the heights of Montmartre above Paris on a summer's evening, suffusing the whole scene in misty blue.

THE
CAPPIELLO EPOCH

Cappiello's era signals both the culmination of the belle epoque and the beginning of its end. He distilled some of the best elements of the past—the caricature approach of Guillaume or Barrère, the simple lines and flat colors of the British school, and a way of making the lettering an integral part of the design which had been practiced by posterists from Chéret to Pal. But in synthesizing them, he came up with something that denied, surpassed, and eventually destroyed the past: simplification that obliterated all the elaborate ornamentation of art nouveau, clarity of vision that obviated the necessity for painstaking details of the pictorial style, and single-mindedness of purpose that eliminated the need for allegorical allusions and mythological references.

Cappiello's posters are there to sell, and they do it by attracting attention to the advertised product. Like his predecessors, Cappiello used mostly women as his subjects—but they are purely two-dimensional beings, with no pretense to flesh-and-blood sensuality. They represent feminine allure but do not possess it themselves: it is a synthetic attraction, but it is all the more effective because it does not depend on an individual's reaction to a specific face or figure. A Cappiello woman does not remind us of any particular person: she is any woman, and what attracts us is the bold and brazen way in which she insinuates herself into our consciousness. Cappiello had the temerity to try to sell a product which he doesn't show by the image of a woman with no discernible facial features riding a horse which, being bright red, is obviously not of this world. The fact that it worked spectacularly well started a whole new trend in posters, and in advertising in general: Cappiello became the father of modern advertising.

Today, of course, concepts like surrealism, abstraction, synthesis are old hat. We must remember, however, that in the era of Victorian conservatism, Cappiello's flights of fancy must have been like a fresh breeze—or, perhaps more likely, a hurricane—that swept up all the old-fashioned ideas into a sorry heap. The old *new* art is dead—long live the new *new* art!

LEONETTO CAPPIELLO

Born in the Italian resort town of Livorno, Cappiello (1875–1942) had a natural talent for drawing, and his first ambition was to be a great painter. He started studying art with a painter's career in mind, but meanwhile, purely as a hobby, he would make a quick sketch of anybody who caught his attention—relatives, home town characters, an occasional interesting tourist. Soon, he found that these quick caricatures were always favorably received, and by the time he was 21, he was able to make a little money by having the best of these homespun drawings published in booklet form.

That may not have swayed him in itself, but two years later, in 1898, he took a trip to Paris to visit his older brother who happened to be working there at the Stock Exchange. Leonetto found Paris intoxicating, and wanted to put off returning to his sleepy little seaside hometown for a while; the only way to do it, of course, was by finding a way to support himself.

Why not utilize his gift for caricature again? His brother told him that various magazines might pay a good price for caricatures of celebrities, particularly ones that have not been done to death already. Since that was true of most of the regular Paris stars, Leonetto approached two famous visitors who were just then staying in town, and who, being fellow Italians, might be willing to give an untried kid a break: actor Ermete Novelli and composer Giacomo Puccini. They obliged, and Leonetto promptly sold the sketches to *Le Rire*; they were so well received that within weeks, he became the favored caricaturist of theater and cabaret stars of Paris.

One of the major reasons for the quick acceptance of Cappiello was the fact that his caricatures were never offensive: where other caricaturists would grossly distort their subjects' facial features and hold them up for ridicule, Cappiello used only subtle exaggeration to spotlight their outstanding characteristics. This gave him access to the one group of performers who previously fought tooth and nail not to be caricatured: the prominent ladies of the stage. When they saw that he meant them no harm, even the most famous names of the day—Sarah Bernhardt, Réjane, Jeanne Granier—were suddenly willing to sit still for caricatures, and the young man from Livorno became the darling of the foremost beauties of Paris.

This prompted Alexandre Natanson, co-publisher of *La Revue Blanche*, one of the magazines that had been using his sketches, to commission Cappiello to publish a portfolio of these drawings under the title "Nos Actrices" ("Our Actresses"), which came out in 1899 and launched his career in earnest.

But he might have remained a professional illustrator if one of the editors to whom he routinely submitted sketches had not asked him to prepare a poster for a new humor magazine he was launching, *Le Frou-Frou*. Cappiello used a simple caricature in his usual style—a can-can girl kicking up her skirts—but now he had to use color, so he opted for a plain yellow background and a dab of red on the pantaloons peeking out from under the petticoats.

The poster, prepared so quickly in such an offhand way, made a provocative splash on the billboards that no passer-by could resist. Instinctively, Cappiello hit on the right formula: create an eye-catching character and make a bold, loud statement—and everything else becomes immaterial. It brought him immediate further offers from various advertisers, and made him aware of the enormous power of effective communication: he had found the field in which he would labor for the rest of his life.

His technique evolved fundamentally from that of British posterists like Hassal, Hardy and the Beggarstaff Brothers, who used simple drawings and flat colors—only Cappiello added dynamic zest and dramatic impact they had never dreamed of. The designs, for the first few attempts, are firmly rooted in his caricature style; but gradually, he frees his imagination and begins to develop a poster language even more compelling.

Painting of Cappiello in 1903 by Georges Barbier (Rennert collection).

With a few exceptions, Cappiello used two printer-agents for his work: up to World War I, it was Vercasson, where he developed the principles of his style; after that, it was Devambez, where he continued to apply them with an even greater flair and bolder imagination. The key to his approach was always image association—the idea that you don't really remember the image of the product itself, but the image of something that is associated with the product. Thus, if you are shown the picture of an old-fashioned phonograph with a listening horn, you don't think of any particular brand as it could be any of a dozen names; but if you see a small white dog listening to it attentively, the brand name "RCA Victor" will flash to your mind instantly, involuntarily, because the association had been firmly established there. Cappiello was the first who thoroughly understood this, and he applied it with commendable diligence in about a thousand posters.

He had an active career which lasted approximately 40 years, during which time he produced an average of two posters per month. Although in such quantity it is inevitable that certain themes and concepts are repeated continually, it is to Cappiello's credit that his inventiveness never flagged, and he was always able to come up with new ways to shock us, startle us out of our pedestrian complacency, and ultimately delight us.

157.
Leonetto Cappiello
BACCHANAL
1908: original design
17½ x 23½ in./44.4 x 59.8 cm

158. ▶
Leonetto Cappiello
CHAMPAGNE
DELBECK
1902: Vercasson, Paris
37⅜ x 52⅞ in./95 x 134.3 cm
Cap/GP, 245
PAI-VI, 39

Cappiello was the favorite posterist of the French and Italian liquor industry for whom he did more than hundred posters; some of the top brands—Cinzano, Gancia, Campari, Marie Brizard—were repeat clients. No doubt the merry BACCHANAL, a preliminary design found in his estate, was meant for one of them, or possibly for an institutional ad for the wine growers.

The poster for CHAMPAGNE DELBECK features a stunning blonde in an orange dress who winces a little as she pops the cork—a typically exuberant Cappiello moment.

CHAMPAGNE

DELBECK
REIMS

IMP VERCASSON & C.ⁱᵉ, 43 Rue de Lancry, PARIS

ELIXIR PERUVIEN

159.
Leonetto Cappiello
ELIXIR PERUVIEN
1902: original design
39 x 57¼ in. / 99 x 145.5 cm

160. ▶
Leoneto Cappiello
PUR CHAMPAGNE/
DAMERY-EPERNAY
1902: Vercasson, Paris
38¾ x 52½ in. / 98.5 x 133.4 cm
Cap/GP, 246
PAI-VI, 36

As can be seen from the maquette, the image originally intended for ELIXIR PERUVIEN wound up as an institutional poster for the PUR CHAMPAGNE growers in the Damery-Eper-nay region, the only difference being in the way the girl holds the bottle. Since no poster for the "elixir," by Cappiello or anyone else, has come to our attention, it is possible that the product never reached the marketing stage, and the artist didn't want to waste a dynamic design.

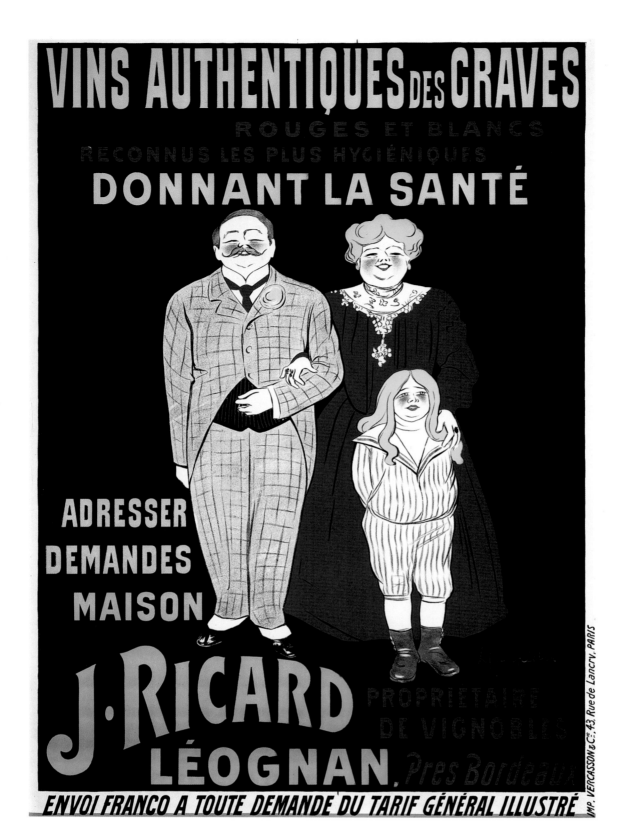

A rarely seen poster for J. RICARD uses an interesting approach, selling the product by associating the winemaker's name with an aura of middle-class prosperity and respectability.

The Ricard family started as wine merchants and distributors in Leognan in the Bordeaux region, and in the late 1800s, Joseph Ricard acquired a few acres of vineyards as well. However, it was his son Paul who created what today is one of the largest corporate entities in the business. Seeing that absinthe could no longer be made after World War I, Paul came up with an aperitif made of aniseed, called Pastis, which he began to market in Marseilles during the 1920s. The huge popular acclaim for this product led to rapid expansion, and in 1974, the merger of Ricard with Pernod created one of the ten largest giants in the French liquor and wine merchandising business.

For CHAMPAGNE DE ROCHEGRE, one of the products of the Chamonard distillery in Epernay, Cappiello has an elegant woman in a formal black dress taking a delicate sip, as if afraid that too much of the bubbly might go to her head.

PROPRIÉTÉ DE LA MAISON J. B. CHAMONARD _ ÉPERNAY
CHAMPAGNE
De ROCHEGRÉ
ÉPERNAY
EXTRA-QUALITY
IMP. P. VERCASSON & Cie, 43, rue de Lancry, PARIS

163.
Leonetto Cappiello
L. SEGOL FILS/GRANDS
CHAIS DU MEDOC
1901: Vercasson, Paris
38¾ x 53¼ in./98.5 x 135.2 cm
DFP-II, 129
Cap/GP, 213
PAI-IX, 6

164. ▶
Leonetto Cappiello
SUC DU VELAY
1902: Vercasson, Paris
38¾ x 54½ in./98.5 x 138.4 cm
PAI-IX, 12

Still in his caricature stage, Cappiello uses known stage personalities in his poster for L. SEGOL FILS: Jeanne Granier and Albert Brasseur. These were not endorsements in today's sense, where the stars get huge sums for being associated with a promotional campaign: the client probably asked permission, possibly sweetening the request with a bottle or two of the product, but in most cases the performers were happy to get the publicity and cooperated gladly. Jeanne Granier (1852-1939) made her debut as a singer at the age of 22, and became one of the favorite interpreters of light comedy roles in Offenbach's operettas. When her voice gave out at 43, she switched effortlessly to legitimate theater, starting with the play "Amants" in 1895. Albert Brasseur (1862-1932) was the son of a comedian, and he followed in his father's footsteps from the ground up, starting with burlesque and working his way up to a fine farceur; for years, he starred at the Variété.

SUC DU VELAY, which always carried the legend "Liqueur des Gourmets" on its bottles, is being offered to us by a blonde in a pea green cape who beckons with a toast.

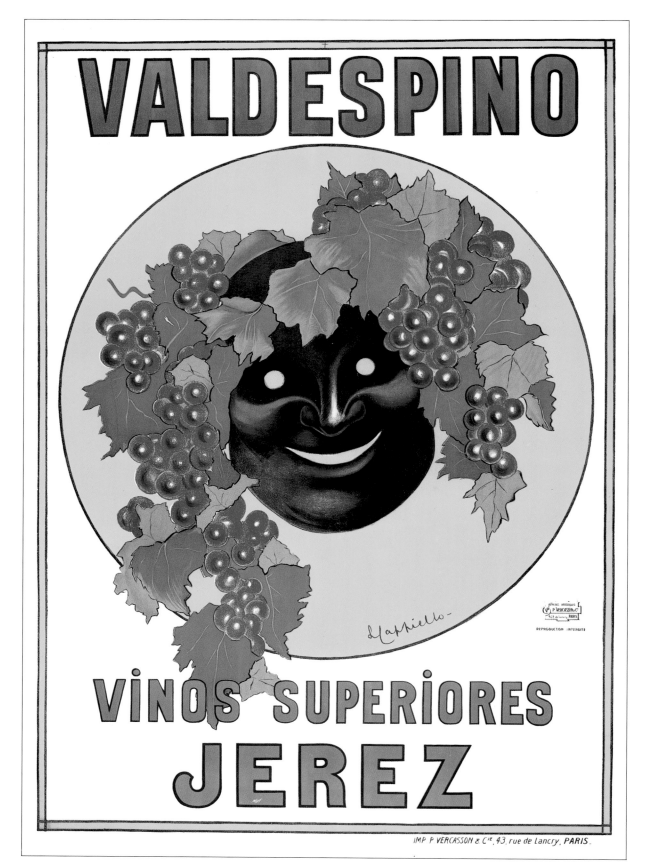

165.
Leonetto Cappiello
VALDESPINO/JEREZ
1906: Vercasson, Paris
37⅞ x 55 in./96.2 x 139 cm
PAI-VI, 54

166. ▶
Leonetto Cappiello
COGNAC FINE
CHAMPAGNE
1905: original design
35½ x 53¼ in./90.1 x 135.2 cm

In VALDESPINO, Cappiello surprises us with a smiling mask wreathed in purple grapes to sell a brand of sherry. He rarely did posters not based on a person, but when he did, it was with the same flair, always choosing something off-beat or startling to catch our eye.

In the maquette for the COGNAC FINE CHAMPAGNE poster, the maid serves the beverage with joyous frivolity; she probably sampled the product on the way. We must bear in mind that in those days of tight corsets, garter belts and bustles, such a light step would be no mean accomplishment; Cappiello's drawings often seem to suggest in a subtle way that women should have more freedom of movement. (See inset for printed poster).

COGNAC PELLISSON

167.
Leonetto Cappiello
COGNAC PELLISSON
1907: Vercasson, Paris
44¾ x 61¼ in./113.7 x 155.6 cm
PAI-VII, 70

168. ▶
Leonetto Cappiello
COGNAC GAUTIER
FRERES
1907: Vercasson, Paris
45⅝ x 62 in./116 x 157.5 cm

In COGNAC PELLISSON, Cappiello is in his element, stunning us with a visual shock: the sheer incongruity of a red-headed imp carrying a monstrous barrel is bound to catch us off balance, and he's got our attention.

A similar disparity in size is also the key to COGNAC GAUTIER, another ocular delight. It advertises the oldest cognac enterprise to survive into the present, established by Guy Gautier in 1697. This was a period in which the increasing demand for French spirits overseas, and the discovery that wines do not survive long sea voyages any too well, led to the development of sturdier liquors such as brandies. Gautier's success was partly due to the fact that he sided with the insurrectionists in one of the religious wars that took place in his time; when they won, he was named governor of the Cognac province, and he in turn passed its name to the brandy he had produced. His son Jean expanded the business to England, and successive generations carried on the family trade to a great prosperity.

COGNAC
GAUTIER FRÈRES
FRANCE
Imp. P. VERCASSON & Cie, 43, Rue de Lancry, PARIS.

169.
Leonetto Cappiello
COGNAC ALBERT
ROBIN
1906: Vercasson, Paris
47¼ x 63 in./120 x 137.2 cm

170. ▶
Leonetto Cappiello
COGNAC DE L'AIGLE
Ca. 1904: Vercasson, Paris
47¼ x 63⅛ in./120 x 137.2 cm

The bird with the colorful plumage is a typical Cappiello ploy to insure that we take a second look. COGNAC ALBERT ROBIN has been manufactured since 1860 by the Charrier family, an important clan in the Cognac district who have been major landowners, vineyard operators and distillers for more than five centuries.

A bird of a different color is COGNAC DE L'AIGLE, a very rare, never before documented strong image. It advertises the Eagle brand of Delamain & Co.'s cognac; from the address of the distributor, it appears that the poster was intended for use in Egypt. One would assume that the poster was made available to other distributors, to insert their own particulars in the allotted space, but so far no other copies have come to light.

A scampering golden faun representing a brandy producer? Cappiello must have been mindful of the fact that the ancient Greek god Pan was always described as half goat, half man, and being a mischievous spirit who enjoyed having a good time, he became the patron saint of revelers and tipplers.

The MARTELL family traces its origin to the 11th century on the island of Jersey; the distillery was established by Jean Martell at Cognac in 1715. Its long-standing trade name, J. & F. Martell, came into use in 1790 when brothers Jean and Frederic took over the reins. Successive generations continued to produce one of the world's best brands of cognac; in 1972, the company went public and reorganized with a corporate structure.

One of the followers of Pan is the frolicker advertising MUGNIER, a liqueur with a wine base flavored with blackberries and cherries. Its manufacture was started in Dijon in 1863 by Frederic Mugnier; by 1891, he was able to expand by building one of the largest distilling facilities in the area.

Cappiello's design owes something to Loie Fuller's dance under multi-colored lights; in another way, it anticipates, by some 50 years, the psychedelic effect of the early rock posters.

173.
Leonetto Cappiello
ABSINTHE GEMPP
PERNOD
1903: Vercasson, Paris
54 x 76⅝ in./137.3 x 194.9 cm
Menegazzi, 393

174. ▶
Leonetto Cappiello
ABSINTHE DUCROS
FILS
1901: Vercasson, Paris
39 x 54½ in./99 x 138.5 cm
Cap/GP, 244
Cap/StV, 4.11
DFP-II, 115
PAI-IX, 2

Two sisters living in Couvet, Switzerland, gave the world a drink that eventually became the symbol of the evils of alcohol: absinthe. The Henriot sisters' intentions were purely altruistic: in 1797, when a retired French major named Dubied passing through their village became ill, they offered him a potion they had been preparing at home for themselves and a few friends for years: an alcoholic punch they flavored with wormwood, a common herb whose root yielded a bitter but highly intoxicating essence. Dubied liked the drink, bought the formula from them, and immediately started commercial production in Couvet; in 1805, as the demand began to mushroom, he set up a new distillery on the French side of the border, in Pontarlier, for his son-in-law Henri-Louis Pernod. Able now to supply all of France without having to pay duty to the Swiss, it was Pernod who really popularized absinthe, eventually establishing a vast empire of a dozen or more companies, all run by various members of the far-flung family.

The ABSINTHE GEMPP PERNOD poster, featuring one of Cappiello's happy beauties, refers to a branch operation set up at Lunel in 1850 for Edouard Pernod, Henri-Louis' son by his first wife; he, in turn, passed it to his son-in-law Charles Gempp in 1880.

Eventually it was established that wormwood, whose Latin name is *artemisia absinthium*, was a potent hallucinogen with too many unpleasant and dangerous side effects, and the making of absinthe was prohibited during World War I. Undaunted, the great-grandchildren of the founder substituted different herbs for flavor, especially anise and fennel, and continued to make the drink under the name Pernod. After merging with the powerful Ricard interests in 1974, Pernod-Ricard became a major marketing force in the spirits business.

ABSINTHE DUCROS FILS was one of the few brands of absinthe made by a firm with no overt ties to the Pernods; it was set up by Alexandre Ducros well to the south of the Pernod domain, in the Rhone River valley. The poster has an exuberant lady all bathed in red, in a windswept pose, happily offering us the product.

175.
Leonetto Cappiello
ABSINTHE J. EDOUARD
PERNOT
1902: Vercasson, Paris
42⅜ x 58⅜ in./107.6 x 148.2 cm
Cap/StV, 4.20
Menegazzi, 394
PAI-IX, 10

176. ▶
Leonetto Cappiello
LA MARQUISETTE
1901: Vercasson, Paris
39¼ x 82 in./99.7 x 208.3 cm
DFP-II, 112
PAI-VII, 78

Using the humorous approach characteristic of his early caricatures, Cappiello depicts a gentleman waiting eagerly, with a smirk, for a young lady's reaction to her first sip of AB-SINTHE J. EDOUARD PERNOT.

A very convivial scene, one woman introducing another to the after-dinner liqueur MAR-QUISETTE, is treated in a humorous but straightforward fashion.

177.
Leonetto Cappiello
TOG QUINQUINA
1905: Vercasson, Paris
38½ x 53⅝ in./97.8 x 136.2 cm

178. ▶
Leonetto Cappiello
CINZANO VERMOUTH
1910: Cinzano, Torino
37⅜ x 53¾ in./95 x 136.5 cm
Cap/GP, 28
Cap/StV, 4.33

If a young lady on a horse could sell chocolate (see No. 199), why couldn't another one sell an aperitif? Here, the motif is Spanish—the girl's dress, the festive harness on the horse—because Perpignan, where the tonic was made, is close to the Spanish border on the Mediterranean side of the Pyrenees. What she and her horse have to do with TOG QUINQUINA is not clear—but it is also quite immaterial. We're already captivated.

For CINZANO, Cappiello expresses his technique in a nutshell: the orange-and-red striped zebra says it all.

The Cinzanos have been prominent burghers of Turin since at least the 16th century; however, what really put them on the map was the license to make brandy, obtained in 1757 by brothers Carlo, Stephano and Giovanni Cinzano. Their first concoction, considered the prototype of vermouth, was distilled from raisins, cinnamon, clove, mugwort and dittany. Over the next century, the product developed gradually, becoming a standard drink of Europe; later, other liquors were added to the line. Cinzano remains a major Italian enterprise whose products are sold in every corner of the world.

CINZANO
VERMOUTH

For MENTHE-PASTILLE, the captivator is the eerie effect of the twilight on the garden statue of a faun—again, the Pan theme is played upon by Cappiello.

In 1885, Emile Giffard, a pharmacist in the city of Angers in the Loire valley, came up with a digestive tonic flavored with peppermint. Its bouquet reminded him of English mint lozenges, and so he called it simply Menthe Pastille (= mint lozenge). The liqueur was well received from the start, and has remained on the market ever since; in 1972, the manufacture was moved to modern facilities at Avrille, and production exceeded a million bottles per year for the first time in 1984.

179.
Leonetto Cappiello
MENTHE-PASTILLE
1906: Vercasson, Paris
49½ x 77⅜ in./125.7 x 196.5 cm
Cap/GP, 269
PAI-IX, 47

MENTHE-PASTILLE
LIQUEUR · E. GIFFARD · ANGERS
IMP. P. VERGASSON & Cie, 43, Rue de Lancry, PARIS.
REPRODUCTION INTERDITE

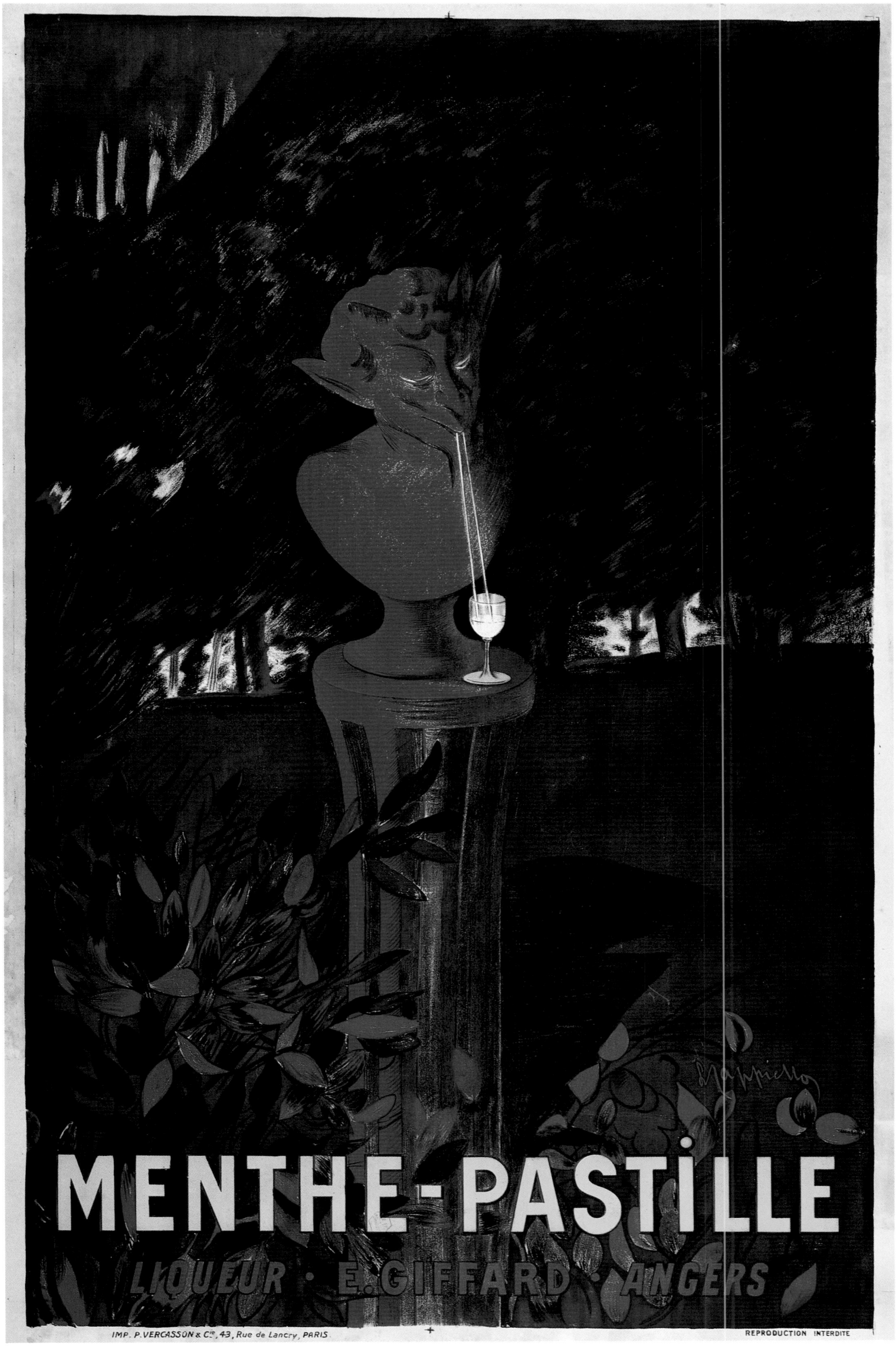

180.
Leonetto Cappiello
ZESTE
1906: Vercasson, Paris
46 x 62½ in./116.9 x 158.7 cm

The ZESTE poster is the first of three designs by Cappiello for the distiller Fournier-Demars; they also asked him to advertise their Triple-Sec in 1907 and their regular Curacao in 1921. The idea of the girl lugging the potted lemon tree is just the sort of thing that awakens our curiosity and forces us, willy-nilly, to pay attention to Cappiello's message.

181.
Leonetto Cappiello
THEATRE DU
VAUDEVILLE—FRERE
JACQUES
1904: Vercasson, Paris
55 x 39½ in./139.6 x 100.3 cm
Cap/GP, 221
DFP-II, 121
PAI-IX, 14

Since the theater was the earliest inspiration and source of income for the young artist, Cappiello frequently prepared posters for theatrical performers and shows in his first few years as a posterist. In them, he clings to a simple caricature style; the elements of shock and fanciful concepts would be out of place, and he rightly eschews it. Although we don't know any of the actors involved, naturally enough, it is still easy to tell that Cappiello's caricatures were a pleasure—piquant, saucy and delectably ribald, always in the very best of taste.

For a comedy FRERE JACQUES at the Théâtre de Vaudeville, Cappiello presents the leading actors: Jeanne Thomassin, Torride and Andrée Mery.

182.
Leonetto Cappiello
FOLIES-BERGERE/
LOUISE BALTHY
1902: Vercasson, Paris
38¾ x 53½ in./98.5 x 136 cm
Cap/GP, 215
Cap/StV, 4.2
PAI-IX, 13

183. ▶
Leonetto Cappiello
FOLIES-BERGERE
1900: Chaix, Paris
36 x 50⅝ in./91.5 x 128.5 cm
Cap/GP, 62
Cap/StV, 4.4
Menegazzi, 73
PAI-IX, 23

A general poster for the FOLIES-BERGERE, here in the printing stage before lettering, was one of four used by the famous music-hall in the year of the Paris World's Fair of 1900. Cappiello chose a variant of the cancan dancer from his FROU-FROU design of a year earlier, still firmly rooted in his caricature style but already a full-fledged poster, with its flat colors and eye-catching dynamics. (See inset for version with text.)

In another design for the FOLIES-BERGERE, we get a likeness of LOUISE BALTHY (1869-1926), a remarkably talented performer who was trained in ballet but broke into show business with comic songs, which secured her an engagement at the Eldorado at the age of 17. A native of Bayonne near the Spanish border, she sometimes affected some Spanish mannerisms, and Cappiello makes it clear in this design. At the time he portrayed her, she was much in demand as a star of lavish revues and spectacles.

IMP. CHAIX (Ateliers Chéret), 20, Rue Bergère, Paris. 17448 8 00 (Encres Lorilleux)

Cappiello - 1900

184.
Leonetto Cappiello
POLAIRE/LE P'TIT
JEUNE HOMME
1903: Vercasson, Paris
39 x 55⅛ in./99 x 140 cm
Cap/GP, 220
PAI-IX, 16

185. ▶
Leonetto Cappiello
ODETTE DULAC
1901: Vercasson, Paris
38 x 53¾ in./96.5 x 136.5 cm
Cap/GP, 212
Cap/StV, 4.3
Menegazzi, 93
PAI-IX, 4

We hardly need to be told that POLAIRE was a striking presence on stage: Cappiello makes that much clear with a few strokes and the choice of a pose and an expression. She was Emilie Bouchaud (1877-1939), originally from Algiers, who was from all accounts quite a character. Endowed by nature with a rather generous bust, she ignored the Victorian dress code which demanded that women conceal their breasts as much as possible, and refused to wear the confining corsets; hence she tended to stand out conspicuously, and it is not beyond conjecture that this may have been at least partly responsible for her entry into show business as a cafe singer at the age of 15. To her credit, she made the most of the opportunity, and seized the very first chance to perform in a stage production; there, she surprised everyone by revealing herself as a sensitive and intelligent comedienne, and within a year was playing soubrette leads in comedies. In 1902, she earned a huge success as the first interpreter of Claudine, the scatter-brained character created by Colette. She also worked in silent comedies for Pathe Films. LE P'TIT JEUNE HOMME opened in May of 1903.

The winsome smile characterized ODETTE DULAC, a performer who went the other way: she started out as an operetta and musical comedy performer, but with this poster she is launching a new career as a cabaret chanteuse. Cappiello gives her a wonderfully pixyish face.

186.
Leonetto Cappiello
HELENE CHAUVIN
1900: Chaix, Paris
35⅜ x 51⅜ in./89.4 x 130.5 cm
DFP-II, 110
PAI-VII, 64

HELENE CHAUVIN is Cappiello's first poster for a stage personality rather than for a specific play or theater. It is not so much a real caricature as what Al Hirschfeld was fond of calling "a character drawing."

187.
Leonetto Cappiello
REJANE/LA
PASSERELLE
1902: Vercasson, Paris
38¼ x 53¾ in./97.2 x 136.7 cm
Cap/GP, 217
Cap/StV, 4.5
PAI-IX, 7

In the poster for the comedy LA PASSERELLE, Cappiello attempted to capture the effervescent quality of RÉJANE, one of the top draws of her day. A contemporary and rival of Sarah
Bernhardt, Réjane—actually Gabrielle Réju (1857-1920)—studied acting at the Conservat-
ory, and made her debut at the Théâtre de Vaudeville; in 1892, she married its director, Mr.
Porel. She tackled any kind of role, from light comedies to classic drama, but proved to be at
her best in playing women of passion: "Madame Sans-Gène," "Zaza," "Sapho." As the creator
of the original Madame Sans-Gène, she got to play her also in the first film version of the famous Sardou piece, made in 1911 for Le Film D'Art.

188.
Leonetto Cappiello
GIL BLAS/
L'IMPOSSIBLE
SINCERITE
1905: Vercasson, Paris
39¾ x 55⅛ in. / 101 x 140 cm
DFP-II, 125

Imp. P. VERCASSON & Cⁱᵉ 43, rue de Lancry, PARIS

189. ▶
Leonetto Cappiello
LE FROU FROU
1899: Lithographie Nouvelle,
Asnières
43¼ x 62¼ in. / 110 x 158 cm
Cap/GP, 207
Cap/StV, 4.1
DFP-II, 109
Menegazzi, 41
Schardt, p. 58
PAI-IX, 22

   An unusual design, with two lovers almost lost in a profusion of red flora, announces the serialization of a novel, L'IMPOSSIBLE SINCERITE, in the magainze GIL BLAS.
   Cappiello's first poster was prepared for a humor magazine about to be launched, LE FROU FROU, at the request of its editor, J. de Gastyne. Cappiello's design tells us the magazine will be lively and impudent; the public bought it, and it ran successfully until the start of World War I; eventually, there was a revival in 1922. Cappiello did quite a few posters for publications in later years, particularly for small regional newspapers; the reputation established with *Le Frou Frou* was evidently the best recommendation.

On his rather infrequent travel posters, Cappiello was not above using a bit of romantic realism for the landscape, as he does in the poster for PORTOFINO-KULM, but the people in it are still the simple-outline, flat-color, two-dimensional beings from his regular style. And yet it works: we sense that man is only an intruder amid the breathtaking splendor of nature.

190.
Leonetto Cappiello
PORTOFINO-KULM
1905: Vercasson, Paris
88⅜ x 65 in./224.4 x 165 cm
Cap/GP, 265
PAI-IX, 36

191. ▶
Leonetto Cappiello
LIVORNO/STAGIONE
BALNEARE
1901: Ricordi, Milano
38⅝ x 55⅜ in./98 x 140.5 cm
Cap/GP, 242
Cap/StV, 4.18
Menegazzi, 180
PAI-V, 119

Cappiello was kept busy by his Parisian clients, and only rarely had time to accept orders from his native country—but LIVORNO was his home town, and he was willing to make an exception. The Japanese lanterns are an inspired idea: they create a festive atmosphere. And it is, after all, a summer festival that is being advertised here.

Cappiello was an acknowledged master of product advertising, because his posters could always stir up excitement. He could do it by various means: often, he would have a fetching young beauty grow ecstatic about the product; at other times, he would use an absurdly far-fetched image association, as stunning as it was daring; on occasion, he would present the product in a startling new way, perhaps an offbeat pattern or geometric exaggeration. But however he did it, his posters always had the vigor necessary to attract attention to themselves and permit the message to reach the audience.

The poster for LA CAISSE SIMON boasts that the "exquisite oysters" packed in the Simon case can reach any destination in Europe still fresh and perfect. In the days before refrigeration or vacuum packing, this was a serious concern; Cappiello depicts a couple testing the validity of the claim as the saleslady opens another sample.

192.
Leonetto Cappiello
LA CAISSE SIMON/
HUÎTRES EXQUISES
1901: Vercasson, Paris
54¼ x 38¼ in./137.9 x 97.1 cm
Cap/GP, 236
Cap/StV, 4.14
DFP-II, 128
Menegazzi, 456
PAI-IX, 34

The young lady munching on an almond biscuit in the AMANDINES DE PROVENCE poster is basically one of his theatrical caricatures, but she conveys her pleasure to us convincingly, and the design does work as a poster; this is one of Cappiello's earliest efforts for Vercasson, a printer-agent who would push him relentlessly, sometimes demanding as many as four posters per month, during their lucrative but oftentimes tempestuous 16-year association.

A later printing of this poster has the bottom line changed to "Biscuits Charles Lalo." Apparently, the firm was taken over by a son or relative.

193. ▶
Leonetto Cappiello
AMANDINES DE
PROVENCE
1900: Vercasson, Paris
39¼ x 55⅛ in./99.8 x 140 cm
Cap/StV, 4.12
Cap/GP, 232
Menegazzi, 444
PAI-II, 137

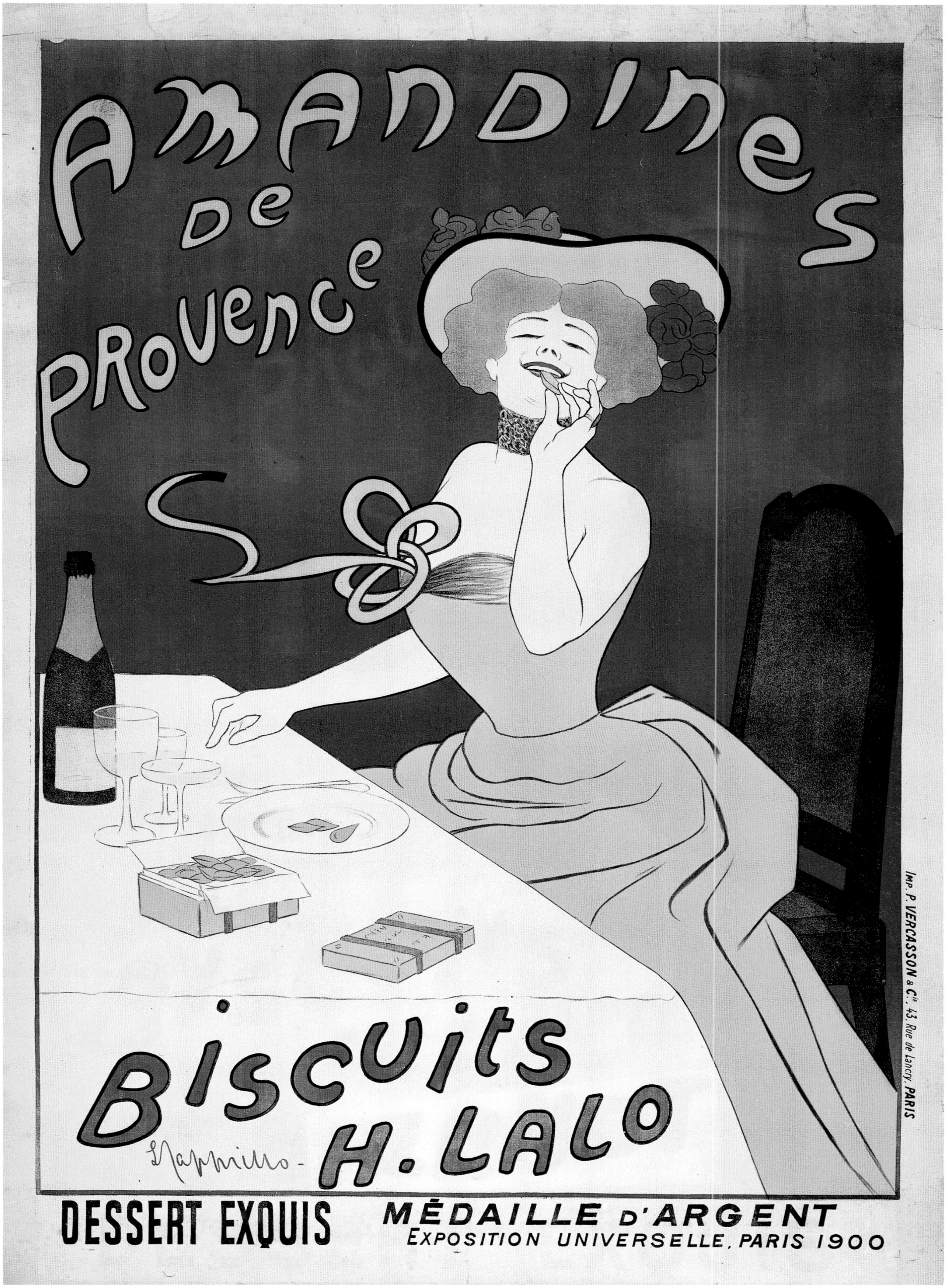
AMANDINES
DE
PROVENCE
BISCUITS
H. LALO
L. Cappiello
Imp. P. VERCASSON & Cie. 43, Rue de Lancry, PARIS
DESSERT EXQUIS
MÉDAILLE D'ARGENT
EXPOSITION UNIVERSELLE, PARIS 1900

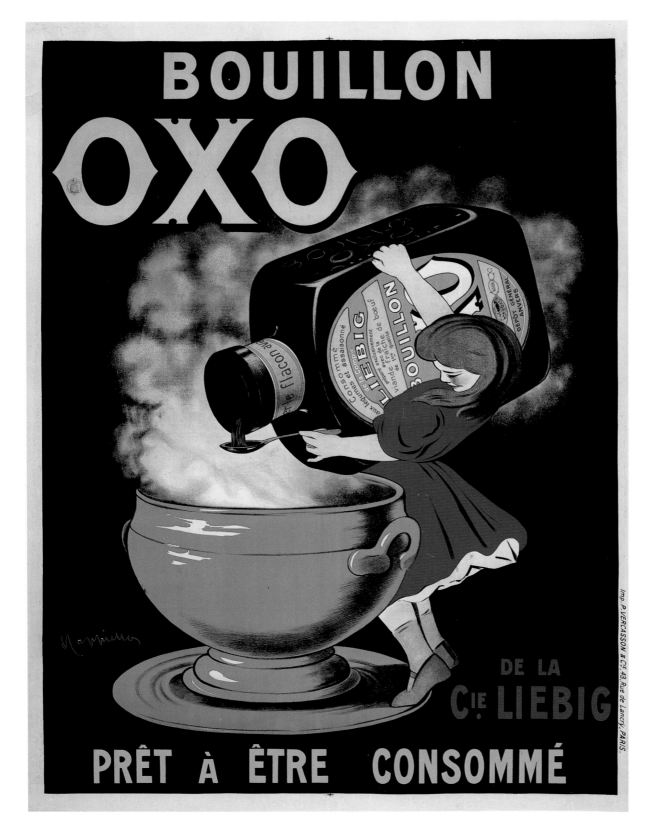

194.
Leonetto Cappiello
BOUILLON OXO
1908: Vercasson, Paris
45¾ x 62 in./116.1 x 157.3 cm
Cap/StV, 4.34

195. ▶
Leonetto Cappiello
PAQUET PERNOT
1905: Vercasson, Paris
42⅝ x 63 in./108.2 x 159.9 cm
Cap/StV, 4.31
PAI-VIII, 285

A good example of an eye-catching trick is to play with the dimensions, and Cappiello employed the technique a number of times, here at its most charming: the idea of the little girl struggling so valiantly with the huge bottle tugs at the heartstrings, and instantly, BOUILLON OXO is associated with a positive, warm and homey image.

PAQUET PERNOT is another poster in which the packaging is stressed even more than the product; apparently, the idea of selling bakery products in boxes rather than fresh off the shelves was still meeting buyer resistance, and it was necessary to convince the public that this was an acceptable way to get fresh tasting biscuits. Cappiello is nothing if not self-indulgent; told to advertise a box, he gives you hundreds of boxes. That way, you can't miss the message if you tried.

◄ 196.
Leonetto Cappiello
FLEUR DES NEIGES
1905: Vercasson, Paris
46 x 62⅝ in./116.9 x 159 cm

Cap/GP, 263
Cap/StV, 4.19
PAI-IX, 21

197.

Leonetto Cappiello
SODAS SCARPATETT
1905: Vercasson, Paris
37¼ x 52¼ in./94.7 x 132.7 cm

FLEUR DES NEIGES is one of the products of Biscuits Pernot; since it means "snow flower," Cappiello creates a verbal association by giving us two lovelies worthy of the name, their red coats like blossoms in the white vastness.

In the SODAS SCARPATETT design, it is the bright, sunny colors that set the tone for a line of soft drinks flavored with fruits from the sunny climates.

The poster for NOUILLES-MACARONIS FERRARI harks back to Cappiello's caricature days, with a whole parade of stars helping to sell pasta. Not content just to associate himself with a dozen music-hall and theater folk, Ferrari also tries to insinuate that he has something to do with the Opera, boasting that his factory is located in the same city. However, his inflated ego did give Cappiello an opportunity to give us a fair sampling of his best caricature style: the performers are Mounet-Sully (Jean Sully), Eve Lavallière (Eugenia Fenoglio), Baron (Jacques de Baroncelli), Jane Hading (Jeanne Trefouret), Coquelin Ainé (Benoit Constant), Réjane (Gabrielle Réju), Albert Brasseur, Charles LeBargy, Jeanne Granier, Lucien Guitry, Coquelin Cadet (Ernest Constant) and Marthe Brandès (Josephine Brunschwig).

198.
Leonetto Cappiello
NOUILLES-
MACARONIS / FERRARI
1904: Vercasson, Paris
62 x 45¾ in. / 157.5 x 116 cm
Cap / GP, 224

199. ▶
Leonetto Cappiello
CHOCOLAT KLAUS
1903: Vercasson, Paris
38 x 54 in. / 96.5 x 137 cm
Cap / GP, 257
Cap / StV, 4.24
DFP-II, 120
Menegazzi, 448
Weill, p. 125
PAI-IX, 37

With the poster for CHOCOLAT KLAUS, Cappiello established himself firmly as the pioneer of the new trend in posters, and indeed in all advertising. From then on, he pursued the principles of visual shock and image association, the cornerstones of sales motivation sciences, with a clarity and determination that set him apart from his colleagues. The major innovation that startled Parisians at the time was not only the outrageous color of the horse, but the total absence of the product. The powerful graphic message is still used by the company nearly a century later, and it still has the same impact.

CHOCOLAT

KLAUS

200.
Leonetto Cappiello
REGLISSE
SANGUINEDE
1902: Vercasson, Paris
38¼ x 53¼ in./97.2 x 135.2 cm
Cap/GP, 253
Cap/StV, 4.7
Menegazzi, 374
DFP-II, 127
PAI-IX, 9

201. ▶
Leonetto Cappiello
LE THERMOGENE
1909: Vercasson, Paris
46⅛ x 62⅜ in./117.2 x 158.4 cm
Cap/GP, 278
Cap/StV, 4.30
Weill, 210
PAI-IX, 45

The well dressed lady is reaching for her cough lozenge REGLISSE SANGUINEDE, flavored with licorice. A charming design in properly subdued winter colors.

The Pierrot figure advertising LE THERMOGENE, a brand of poultice, is one of Cappiello's best known creations. Never mind the claims that Thermogène will keep you warm and cure coughs, rheumatism and cramps; Cappiello's inventive exaggeration will always make you remember the image and associate it with the product—and that's the hallmark of a good poster. The proof is that 80 years later, it is still in use.

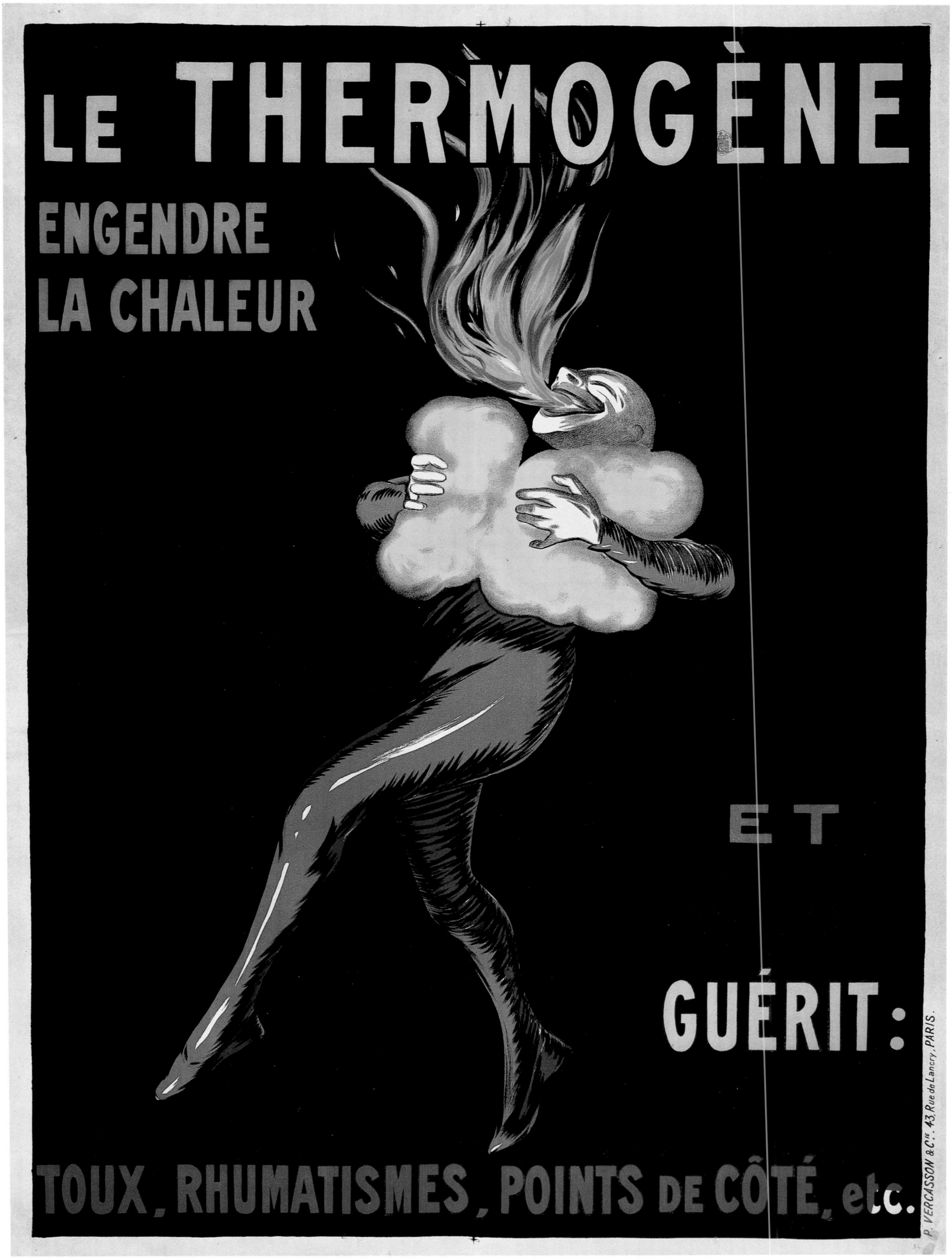
LE THERMOGÈNE
ENGENDRE
LA CHALEUR
ET
GUÉRIT:
TOUX, RHUMATISMES, POINTS DE CÔTÉ, etc.
P. VERCASSON & Cie. 43, Rue de Lancry, PARIS.

INDISPENSABLE AUX FUMEURS

DANS LES BUREAUX DE TABAC ET PHARMACIES

IMP. P. VERCASSON & Cie. 43, Rue de Lancry, PARIS

202.
Leonetto Cappiello
CACHOU LAJAUNIE
1900: Vercasson, Paris
37⅞ x 53¾ in./96.3 x 136.5 cm
Cap/GP, 231
Cap/StV, 4.10
PAI-IX, 52

CACHOU LAJAUNIE is one of Cappiello's very earliest designs for Vercasson—one of only three he did for him in the year 1900, his first full year in the poster business—and yet it remains one of his best. Simple and effective, it has a lovely redhead indulging in a smoke, delighted in the knowledge that her "cachou," a breath sweetener, will obliterate any tell-tale traces of her secret.

203.
Leonetto Cappiello
KATABEXINE
1903: Vercasson, Paris
39 x 54¼ in./99 x 137.7 cm
Cap/GP, 252
Cap/StV, 4.22
DFP-II, 118
Schardt, pp. 174-5
PAI-VII, 63

Three years later, a somewhat bolder design for a similar product, KATABEXINE—a cough tablet soluble in water—features a pretty blonde serving the same function: showing that she is thoroughly happy with the product, confident it will protect her from all winter miseries.

204.
Leonetto Cappiello
LES PARFUMS DE
J. DAVER
1903: Vercasson, Paris
39 x 53⅞ in./99 x 136.7 cm
DFP-II, 126
Menegazzi, 507
PAI-IX, 15

205. ▶
Leonetto Cappiello
PAPIER A CIGARETTES
JOB
1912: Vercasson, Paris
23 x 34⅝ in./58.5 xc 90.5 cm
DFP-II, 124
PAI-IX, 51

A style-conscious lady applies one of LES PARFUMS DE J. DAVER, her smile anticipating its effect on the gentlemen in her life and the compliments she is sure to receive. Note how the fur virtually makes an arrow directing our gaze to the product.

The JOB company made cigarette paper, later adding a line of cigarettes, and it always used top artists to create posters for its products, including Mucha (No. 74), Atché (No. 101) and others. Cappiello chooses to go for the surprise, using everybody's idea of an Oriental potentate to create an incongruous, and therefore memorable, image association.

PAPIER à CIGARETTES

JOB

13ᵐᵉ ÉDITION JUIN 1933 IMPRIMERIE ÉTABLᵗ VERCASSON 6.RUE MARTEL PUBLICITÉ PARIS

206.
Leonetto Cappiello
E. & A. MELE & CI
MASSIMO BUON
MERCATO
1902: Ricordi, Milano
59⅛ x 81⅜ in./150.2 x 206.7 cm
PAI-IV, 9

The Naples department store E. & A. MELE was important in the development of Italian poster art, as it consistently used prominent artists for its outdoor advertising, which was among the most lavish for any type of store anywhere. By always showing the latest in fashion trends, Mele—whose prices were quite reasonable—made a wide public style-conscious; these images made the ordinary people, who knew they could afford to shop at Mele's, aspire to the elegance and sophistication shown in the store's posters. The challenge for the posterists

207.
Leonetto Cappiello
E. & A. MELE & CI
NOVITA PER
SIGNORA
1903: Ricordi, Milano
59⅜ x 80⅜ in./150 x 205 cm
Menegazzi, 475
PAI-IV, 10

was to show that anyone could look great with a little effort—and this led to the development of a poster style dubbed "bourgeois realism." All the best known names in Italian posters worked for Mele at one time or another—Metlicovitz, Dudovich, Malerba, Laskoff—and even expatriate Cappiello could not escape. His two contributions give the message perfectly: you, too, can look like a million with clothes from Mele's.

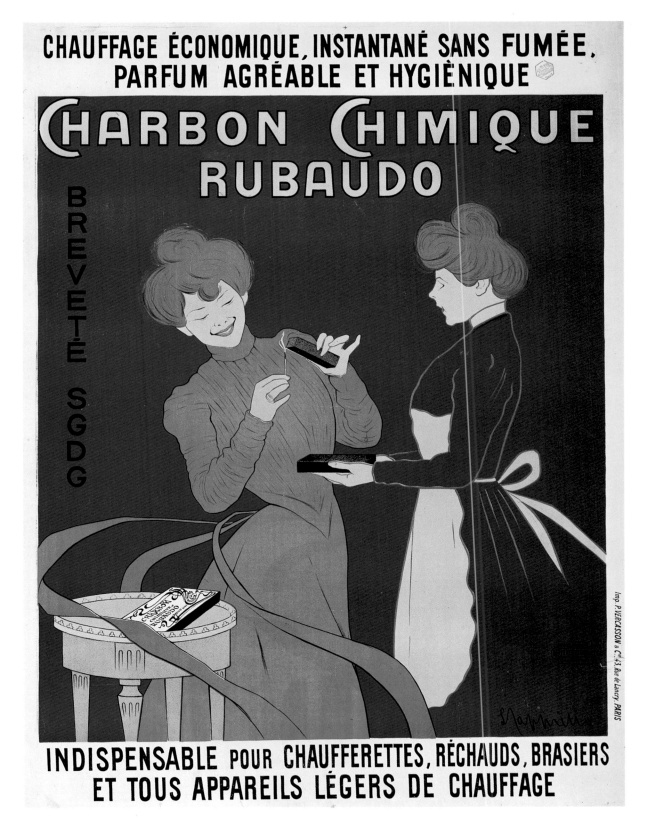

CHAUFFAGE ÉCONOMIQUE, INSTANTANÉ SANS FUMÉE, PARFUM AGRÉABLE ET HYGIÈNIQUE

CHARBON CHIMIQUE RUBAUDO

BREVETÉ SGDG

INDISPENSABLE POUR CHAUFFERETTES, RÉCHAUDS, BRASIERS ET TOUS APPAREILS LÉGERS DE CHAUFFAGE

Imp. P. VERCASSON & Cⁱᵉ, 43, Rue de Lancry, PARIS

The basic message of a jeweler like COLIN is, of course, that a little sparkle can go a long way. How to show this graphically? Cappiello does the design in black, and shows how a touch of gold here and green there does make a conspicuous difference: a textbook solution to a design problem.

CHARBON CHIMIQUE RUBAUDO is as drab as a product gets: plain charcoal briquets used for lighting fires. Since the idea is that they will bring you warmth, Cappiello bathes everything in a warm red; then he shows the ease of handling by having the woman of the house insist on having the personal pleasure of touching a match to the product, rather than having the maid do it. Presto, the dull product is dull no more.

HYGIÈNE, ÉLÉGANCE, SOUPLESSE

CORSET
LE FURET

BREVETÉ S.G.D.G.

maintient mais ne comprime pas

Donne la Souplesse de l'Orientale avec la grâce Française

Imp. P. VERCASSON & Cie, 43, rue de Lancry, PARIS

210.
Leonetto Cappiello
CORSET LE FURET
1901: Vercasson, Paris
38⅜ x 54⅞ in./97.5 x 139.4 cm
Cap/GP, 237
Cap/StV, 4.8
Menegazzi, 465
PAI-VII, 66

211. ▶
Leonetto Cappiello
CHAUSSURES J. B.
TORRILHON
1906: Vercasson, Paris
39¼ x 55 in./99.7 x 139.7 cm
Cap/GP, 268

The shapely young lady admires her form, presumably much enhanced by CORSET LE FURET; in Vercasson's publicity, there was a letter from the director of the company stating that the design "exceeded our expectations" and "contributed to the popularization of our trademark." What posterist could ask for a better recognition of his talents?

One of Cappiello's wonderful, irresistible excesses, the cute little frog advertising TORRILHON rubbers is imaginative advertising at its very best. Other than the name of the product, nothing more is said; nothing more is needed.

212.
Leonetto Cappiello
AUTOMOBILES
BRASIER
1906: Vercasson, Paris
47 x 62½ in./119.4 x 159 cm
Cap/GP, 272
Cap/StV, 4.28
PAI-IX, 46

Cappiello's genius for the unorthodox is quite clearly indicated in the poster for AU-TOMOBILES BRASIER. Let's show that this car goes so fast it leaves everything behind it in the dust—and while we're at it, what's wrong with making the dust a swirl of rainbow colors? No one coming across it for the first time can overlook it—especially since it also came in a very large size for billboard purposes.

REFERENCES

The abbreviated references on the left side are those used in the captions for each poster as well as in the text where quoted.

Abdy
French Poster by Jane Abdy. Clarkson N. Potter, New York, 1969

Adhémar
Toulouse-Lautrec. Lithographies-Pointes Sèches-Oeuvre Complet by Jean Adhémar. Arts et Métiers Graphiques, Paris, 1965. (English language edition, *Toulouse-Lautrec—His Complete Lithographs and Drypoints*, published by Harry N. Abrams, New York, 1965).

Adriani
Toulouse-Lautrec: The Complete Graphic Works,, by Gotz Adriani. The catalogue raisonne, featuring the Gerstenberg collection. Thames & Hudson, London, 1988.

Affichomanie
L'Affichomanie. Catalogue of the exhibition on the subject of the postermania of the period 1880–1900 held at the Musée de l'Affiche, Paris, 1980. Text by Alain Weill, curator.

Arwas
Berthon & Grasset by Victor Arwas. Academy Editions, London; Rizzoli, New York, 1978.

Bargiel & Zagrodzki
Steinlen-Affichiste. Catalogue Raisonné, by Réjane Bargiel and Christophe Zagrodzki. Editions du Grand-Pont, Lausanne, 1986. (Distributed in the United States by Posters Please, Inc., New York City).

Beaumont
L'Affiche Belge, by A. Demeure de Beaumont. Published by the author. Toulouse, France, 1897.

Belgische Affiche
De Belgische Affiche 1900. Belgian posters from the period 1892–1914, by Yolande Oostens-Wittamer. Text in Flemish. Koningklijke Bibliotheek Albert I, Brussels, 1975.

Belle Epoque 1970
La BelleEpoque—Belgian Posters. The catalogue-book of the touring exhibition of the Wittamer-DeCamps collection. Text by Yolande Oostens Wittamer. Grossman Publishers, New York, 1971.

Belle Epoque 1980
La Belle Epoque. Catalogue of the loan exhibition from the Wittamer-DeCamps collection, featuring the works of Combaz, Léo Jo and Livemont. Text by Yolande Oostens-Wittamer. International Exhibitions Foundation, 1980–81

Boissons
Les Boissons/Un Siècle de Réclames, by F. Ghozland. Editions Milan, Toulouse, 1986.

Broido
The Posters of Jules Chéret: 46 Full color Plates and an Illustrated Check List, by Lucy Broido. Dover Publications, N.Y., 1980.

Cap/GP
Cappiello. Catalogue of the exhibition at the Galerie Nationale du Grand Palais in Paris, 1981.

Cap/StV
Leonetto Cappiello—dalla pittura alla grafica. Catalogue of the exhibition in Centro Culturale Saint-Vincent. Text by Raffaele Monti and Elisabeth Matucci. Artificio, Firenze, 1985.

Coll. Lendl
Alphonse Mucha: La Collection Ivan Lendl. Catalogue of the exhibition at Musée de la Publicité, Paris, 1989. Text by Jack Rennert. Editions Syros/Alternatives, Paris.

Conrad
Absinthe, by Barnaby Conrad III. Chronicle Books, San Francisco, 1988.

Crauzat
L'Oeuvre Gravé et Lithographié de Steinlen, by E. de Crauzat. Société de Propagation des Livres d'Art, Paris, 1913.

DFP-II
Das Frühe Plakat in Europa und den USA. Vol. II. French and Belgian Posters. Edited by Ruth Malhotra, Marjan Rinkleff and Bernd Schalicke. Mann Verlag, Berlin, 1977.

Delteil
Le Peintre-Graveur Illustré, by Loys Delteil. (Volumes X and XI devoted to Toulouse-Lautrec.) Paris, 1920. Reprinted by Collectors Edition Ltd.-Da Capo Press, New York, 1969.

Folies-Bergère
100 Years of Posters of the Folies-Bergère and Music Halls of Paris, by Alain Weill. Images Graphiques, New York, 1977.

French Opera
French Opera Posters 1868–1930, by Lucy Broido. Dover Publications, New York, 1976.

Hiatt
Picture Posters, by Charles Hiatt. George Bell and Sons, London, 1895.

Hillier
Posters, by Bevis Hillier. Weidenfeld and Nicholson, London, 1969; Stein & Day, New York, 1969; Spring Books, The Hamlyn Publishing Group, New York, 1974.

Livre de l'Affiche
Le Livre de l'Affiche, by Réjane Bargiel-Harry and Christophe Zagrodzki. A publication of the Musée de la Publicité, Paris. Editions Alternatives, Paris, 1985.

Maindron
Les Affiches Illustrées, 1886–1895, by Ernest Maindron. G. Boudet, Paris, 1896.

Maitres
Les Maîtres de l'Affiche 1896–1900, by Roger Marx. Imprimerie Chaix, Paris 1896–1900. Reprinted as *Masters of the Poster 1896–1900* by Images Graphiques, New York, 1977.

Menegazzi	*Il Manifesto Italiano*, by Luigi Menegazzi. Electa Edsitrice, Milan (ca.1976).
PAI-I	*Premier Posters*. Book of the auction held in New York, March 9, 1985, by Poster Auctions International. Text by Jack Rennert.
PAI-II	*Prize Posters*. Book of the auction held in Chicago, November 10, 1986, by Poster Auctions International. Text by Jack Rennert.
PAI-III	*Poster Impressions*. Book of the auction held in New York, June 1, 1986, by Poster Auctions INternational. Text by Jack Rennert.
PAI-IV	*Prestige Posters*. Book of the auction held in New York, May 3, 1987, by Poster Auctions International. Text by Jack Rennert.
PAI-V	*Poster Pizzazz*. Book of the auction held in Universal City, California, November 22, 1987, by Poster Auctions International. Text by Jack Rennert.
PAI-VI	*Poster Splendor*. Book of the auction held in New York, May 1, 1988, by Poster Auctions International. Text by Jack Rennert.
PAI-VII	*Poster Potpourri*. Book of the auction held in New York, November 13, 1988, by Poster Auctions International. Text by Jack Rennert.
PAI-VIII	*Poster Treasures*. Book of the auction held in New York, May 7, 1989, by Poster Auctions International. Text by Jack Rennert.
PAI-IX	*Poster Palette*. Book of the auction held in New York, November 12, 1989, by Poster Auctions International. Text by Jack Rennert.
Phillips V	*100 Poster Masterpieces*. The catalogue of the Phillips Auction, held May 2, 1981, in New York. Text by Jack Rennert.
Price	*Posters*, by Charles Matlack Price. George W. Bricka, New York, 1913.
R-W	*Alphonse Mucha: The Complete Posters and Panels* by Jack Rennert and Alain Weill. G. K. Hall, Boston, 1984.
Rassenfosse	*Armand Rassenfosse*, by Marie-Laurence Bernard and Victor Henrard. Claude Van Loock, Bruxelles, 1989.
Reims	*Exposition d'Affiches Artistiques Françaises et Etrangères*. The catalogue of the November 1896 exhibition held in Reims. Reissued in a numbered edition of 1,000 copies by the Musée de l'Affiche in 1980. Exclusive distributor in the United States: Posters Please, Inc., New York.
Rennert	*100 Years of Bicycle Posters*, by Jack Rennert. Harper & Row, New York, 1973.
Schardt	*Paris 1900,* by Hermann Schardt. G. P. Putnam's Sons, New York, 1970; reprinted in 1987 by Portland House, New York. (Originally published as *Paris 1900: Französische Plakatkunst*, Belser Verlag, Stuttgart, 1968.)
Wallonie	*L'Affiche en Wallonie. A travers les collections du Musée de la Vie Wallonne*. Edited by the students of the Seminaire d'Esthetique de l'Université de Liége, 1980.
Weill	*The Poster: A Worldwide Survey and History*, by Alain Weill. G. K. Hall, Boston, 1985.
Wember	*Die Jugend der Plakate 1887–1917*, by Paul Wember. Scherpe Verlag, Krefeld, 1961.
Wittrock	*Toulouse-Lautrec: The Complete Prints*, by Wolfgang Wittrock. 2 volumes. Sotheby's, London, 1985.

INDEX

INDEX